IN THE TWILIGHT

IN THE TWILIGHT

ANDRÉ L. SIMON

LONDON
MICHAEL JOSEPH
1969

Pour Jeanne
ma fille aînée et bien-aimée

© ANDRÉ L. SIMON 1969
PRINTED IN GREAT BRITAIN
AT THE CURWEN PRESS, PLAISTOW, E13
SBN NO. 7181 0577X

I wish to record my grateful appreciation
of the most valuable help given to me,
in my near blindness,
by my young and dear friend, Hugh Johnson,
who has seen this book through the press

CONTENTS

I. IN THE BEGINNING

THIS IS 16 July 1968, at Little Hedgecourt—a cold and wet day of an English summer at its worst! My arch-enemies, brambles and woodbine, have nothing to fear from me today! But I have lived much too long in England to let a wet day depress me!

In *By Request* I recorded the main happenings of the first eighty years of my life, but I am sure that I shall have more fun and pleasure in recording now and then, when in the mood, what I may still remember of friends with whom I enjoyed good wine or simply a good time. Most, if not actually all my old friends, and the old wines which we discussed together with such enthusiasm long ago, are no more, but their memory is all the dearer to me. Whether such reminiscences may or may not be published is a matter which does not really concern me. To live again days of long ago with those whom I loved will be for me sufficient reason to put pen to paper.

There is no need, of course, to look far back for happy thoughts! A few days ago—last week—my dearly beloved daughter Jeanne and I enjoyed an excellent lunch at the Vintners' Hall in London with Bruce Todd, the Master, and the other Members of the Court, when we were given their last bottles of Château Latour 1929. Before the lunch, however, something of far greater importance had taken place: I had been made an Honorary Freeman of the Vintners' Company, the first non-English Freeman in the course of the many centuries of the Company's existence! The ceremony started with the Clerk of the Company reading what would have made me blush had I read it as my obituary notice in *The Times*! He had nothing but praise for the evening classes or lectures to the Wine Trade employees, which I gave single handed at Vintners' Hall before 1914—the first-ever attempt at something like technical education in the Wine Trade!

Let the drizzle turn to real rain, and the brambles lap it up! I do not care! A great question mark has just hit my old brain! I had a wife and five young children before 1914; I had little money but a lot to do; my job was to sell my firm's Champagne not only in London but in all parts of the British Isles, not counting two business trips to South America, in 1907 and 1910. The question which now worries me is: Why and how did I give those lectures, which must have demanded a great deal of time and work, without the hope of any financial reward whatsoever?

I cannot remember ever asking myself this question, although it is by no means the first time that I must have had the chance and the time to do so! My memory is no longer as reliable as it used to be; it is so patchy. It is up to me to piece together the bits and pieces which I remember into a picture that will be true in the main, whatever details may be missing!

My father was an artist and my mother was the daughter also of an artist—Emile Dardoize; two of my brothers, Jacques and Maxime, were artists, but I have never been able to draw a straight line, with or without a ruler. No luck! Jacques and I were born in the rue Taranne, he in December 1875, and I on 28 February 1877. The rue Taranne was a short, narrow street starting where the rue de Rennes ended—it came from the Gare Montparnasse to the Boulevard St. Germain. In 1878, all the houses on rue Taranne's right were pulled down and replaced by a pavement and two rows of trees, which are still there, and so is the house where I was born, because it was on the left; it is now in the Boulevard St. Germain.

My brother Roger, number three, was born at Chenonceaux, at a time when my father was painting the murals of the Château's upper gallery. The Château belonged at the time to Madame Pelouse, the wealthy widow of the man who first lit the streets of Paris with *réverbères*, or lamp posts. My other three brothers and my sister were born in rue Coetlogon, in a house adjoining the 92 rue de Rennes house, which was built for my father by Farmuge, one of the architects of the present Paris Hôtel de Ville. The Farmuge family lived on the third floor, we lived on the fourth floor, and my father's studio occupied what might have been the fifth and sixth floors. The No. 4 rue Coetlogon was the family Paris home of two generations of our family. But we also had a house by the sea for the summer, at Carolles.

Carolles is a village on the old Granville–Avranches coach road; in Normandy—but only just. Beyond Avranches, one soon comes to the little Couesnon river which separates Normandy from Brittany. A mile or so from Carolles church and village, there is the *falaise*, the great rocky cliff that faces Cancale, on the other side of the wide sea which may well be called the entry to the Bay of Mont St. Michel. All there was on the wind-swept top of the *falaise*, when I was born, and for many years after, was a small coastguard shelter, on the tip of the cliff, and a very tall blue granite cross a little inland. It was between those two that my father had a house built, in 1880, and this was how and why the whole family came from Paris to Carolles every summer during my father's lifetime. I know that 1880 is the right date because it was carved on one of the walls of the house.

I cannot remember whether I fell down the *falaise*, or how else it happened, but I must have hurt my spine. I do remember that when the rest of the family went back to Paris, at the end of the summer, in 1883 or 1884, I was left at Carolles with my mother, and Dr. and Madame Viollet. Dr. Viollet was a Paris doctor and an old friend of my *Grand père* Dardoize, my mother's father. Every day I was laid down on the dining-room table, firmly held down whilst

Dr. Viollet did his best to reset, massage or iron out my
injured spine. Of course, it hurt a lot and I hated him, but
from the day I reached the age of reason to this very moment, when I am writing about him, I have blessed the
memory of Dr. Viollet. He was the first and maybe the best
of all my good friends; without his skill and devotion, I
would have been a cripple for life!

For some time after that accident, I had to wear a
specially made sort of corset, with a steel or leather support
for the spine, and I was not allowed to run and take part in
any of the usual more or less rough games. However, I was
by no means miserable! I could read and I did read and this
is obviously how books became my first love. Nevertheless,
during that period, which fortunately was not too long, I
must have felt the odd boy out and I became used to keeping my own thoughts to myself rather than being as
articulate as most boys are. Whether any lack of will or
opportunities to speak out had anything to do or not with
my wish to write I cannot tell, but I do remember that my
ambition to be a writer some day was both very early and
quite definite, and, as it happened, the first money that I
ever earned, on leaving school, was as a journalist! The
first school I went to was the Ecole Bossuet, rue Madame,
near the rue Coetlogon. I never could forget how unkind
fate was to me there. On the day of the first *Classe de dessin*
(drawing class) of my first term, there was a plaster head
of Socrates on the platform, also a blackboard and a Professor in an armchair. The boys were given a big sheet of
white paper, a stiff piece of cardboard of the same size, and a
charcoal crayon to draw Socrates' plaster head. The professor had evidently been given a list with the names of the
boys in the class. Of course my name was there, and the
Professor called me up and asked me: 'Are you a son of
Ernest Simon?' I admitted it. 'Then you must be a grandson of my friend Emile Dardoize,' said the Professor, and
I did not deny it, although I did not see what difference it

could make to him. I soon realized, however, that it made
all the difference to me. He told me to take a piece of chalk
and to draw Socrates' head on the blackboard. I can recall
that, hot and bothered as I was, I did my best, but it made
all the boys titter or laugh—and I was punished without
knowing why. I have forgotten what the punishment was
but I still remember the feeling of injustice. Curiously
enough, it did not end there. My grandmother Dardoize
knew Alphonse Daudet and his wife very well, and one day,
as she was lunching with them, she asked Madame Daudet
if I could come with her, and I did. Alphonse Daudet, in a
smiling and very friendly fashion, said to me 'Ah, André
le farceur (joker)' and I didn't know why. I remember that
we had *écrevisse* (crayfish) for lunch because I had never
seen any before, and because Alphonse Daudet, next to
whom I sat, told me to watch him and use my fingers, just
as he did, to eat the little red creatures; it was also the first
time I had been told to take anything out of a soup plate
with my fingers. It was a red letter day for me, but what
kept me awake that night was the *'farceur'*—until it
dawned on me that Lucien Daudet, the author's youngest
son, and much younger than Leon Daudet, his big brother,
was in my class at Bossuet, and that he and probably all the
boys had taken for granted that my caricature of Socrates'
plaster head on the blackboard was a joke. It was not!

After Bossuet, I spent six years at the Petit Seminaire
in the Notre Dame des Champs, where I was never really
happy, and where I never made any real friends. My back
was quite right by this time, but I was not much good at
games; I liked books better, which meant that I was not the
type of boy likely to be popular. What was as regrettable,
if not more regrettable, was the fact that the teaching staff
must have had a poor opinion of my intelligence. At all
exams I was as good as others, maybe better than some, for
the written part, but I always failed at the oral part. The
answer to any question might be perfectly well known to me,

but it stuck in my throat and refused to come out. Just
nerves! I was very glad to leave school and very glad to be
offered near-literary work by a friend of my father's, a
former Zouave Pontifical called Petit de Meurville. He was
at that time literary critic of the Paris *Figaro*, but he was
also publishing, as a hobby I believe, *L'Avant Garde*,
although he found it more and more difficult to find time
for it; this was why he had asked me to work for him.

We published letters from General Baron de Charette to
his former Zouaves Pontificaux, and a number of letters
to the Editor from readers full of grievances against the
Republican regime. Nothing really of any value, and no
advertisements. Which is why *L'Avant Garde* and my
journalistic career were short-lived!

Then came my *service militaire*: three years of the most
unmilitary service that ever was! In those days, a young man
who did not wait to be called up at 21, but volunteered for
three years when 19 or 20, was given the privilege of choosing
the unit in which to serve. So, in 1896, at 19, I volunteered
and chose the 13th Régiment d'Artillerie, at Vincennes,
near Paris. The supreme chief of all French gunners and
gunnery, at the French War Office in Paris at the time,
happened to be Général Deloye. He and his family spent
their summers at Carolles, as we did, and we were friends
of long standing. Général Deloye knew me and knew also
of my love for languages—German, Spanish and Russian,
besides English. I had not been long at Vincennes (where
they dressed me as a French gunner should be dressed)
when an order came from Général Deloye that I was to be
transferred from Vincennes to the Ecole Militaire barracks,
in Paris, which became my official military home for three
years! During the three years of my military service, I
served on the staff of the *Revue d'Artillerie*, by St. Thomas
d'Aquin church, just off the Boulevard St. Germain and the
rue du Bac! The *Revue d'Artillerie* was an official publication sent every month to every French Artillery officer

whether in France or any of the many parts of the world which were at the time under French rule or protection. Its size was the same as that of the *Wine and Food* Magazine from March 1934 to June 1963, that is during the years when I owned and published it! There was an official part with which I had nothing to do: it gave the posting, promotions, deaths and decorations of Artillery officers. The other part, which was a great deal more bulky, gave all manner of information likely to be of some interest to Artillery officers, young and old. All military or near-military books and magazines published in England, the U.S.A., Germany, Russia, and Spain were sent by the War Office Information Department to the *Revue d'Artillerie*, and my job was to look through them and translate anything that I supposed might be of sufficient interest to be published in our magazine. It was then for Capitaine Benoist, the Editor, to decide. I had, of course, a great deal to do, and I probably worked longer hours than anybody else in the whole Regiment, but it was the kind of work which I liked. The morning after the last day of my somewhat unmilitary military service, I left Paris for Reims, where a high stool was given to me to sit at a high desk in the office of Pommery, rue Vauthier-le-Noir. Very dull! I asked and obtained permission to be sent to the Cellars and in 1899 went through a thorough cellarman's apprenticeship. The next year, 1900, I was married, in London, and returned with my bride to Reims for the rest of her and my life, as we both thought at the time. But it was not to be. In 1902, when I was given the chance to go to the firm's London office, I took it and I never regretted it.

Some time in 1903, meeting A. S. Gardiner, who was then the Editor of the *Wine Trade Review*, at Arthur Spencer's office, I casually remarked that I had called myself a journalist once, and that my ambition had been to be a writer, but that must now be forgotten; I had a wife and two babies at home and I had to sell Champagne.

'Nonsense,' said Gardiner. 'You cannot sell any more than drink Champagne all day. If you were born a writer, the urge to write will be with you all your life, and you will never be really happy unless you write. As it happens, you could find time, I am sure, to write as well as sell Champagne.' 'That may be,' I said, 'but nobody in England can be expected to take any interest in what a Frenchman had written.' 'You are quite wrong,' rejoined Gardiner, 'and to prove that I mean it, I am quite willing to publish in the *Wine Trade Review*, in 1904, twelve articles on Champagne, to be paid for at our usual rates.' What a surprise! What a tonic! What a problem! Of course, I knew the names of some of the best vineyards of Champagne, but how many people cared about that in England? I knew how Champagne was bottled and became sparkling, but who did not know that in the wine trade? That was about all I knew about Champagne, and I wished I knew how and when Champagne was first known in England. None of the men in the Wine Trade knew and very few cared! The more hopeless the outlook, the more determined I was not to be beaten, and Gardiner had the twelve articles which he had asked for, for the *Wine Trade Review*, in 1904. They were published in book form, in 1905, as *A History of the Champagne Trade in England*; not a good book, of course, but the first of at least a hundred other books, most of them about wine and/or food, a few about entirely different subjects, in French, and one of them, my best seller, *Laurie's Elementary Russian Grammar*, published by Werner Laurie at the 'elementary' price of sevenpence per copy! The whole print was taken by the War Office and every man who was sent or was meant to be sent to Russia had a copy of my book in his pack!

In my quest for information about the table manners, the food and drink habits of the English in olden times, I had found very little about Champagne, but a great deal about all kinds of other wines which had been known in England for centuries before Champagne had ever been heard of. The Librarian of the Guildhall Library, a friend of A. S. Gardiner who became my friend, thanks to Gardiner, was of great help to me in the choice of the right books. I became so interested, I might even say fascinated with the subject, that I wrote and published, between 1906 and 1909, the three thick volumes of *A History of the Wine Trade in England from the Roman occupation to the end of the Seventeenth Century*—much the best of all my books. But the Wine Trade was not interested!

I could not understand why there was so much ignorance and apathy among so many of the older wine-merchants. It did not only puzzle me; it irritated me! When we of the younger generation founded the Wine Trade Club, in 1908, I suggested that we should have an Education Committee that would give lectures about Wine to the Members. It was agreed, and I was elected Chairman with *carte blanche* to go ahead. There had been no other candidate to be Chairman of the Committee, nor would any other member be willing to be deputy chairman! But what was far more important and alarming was the fact that there was nobody among our Members or the staff of any of the firms in which we served who was willing to come forward and give us talks or lectures! Something had to be done about it, and it was obviously for the Chairman of the Education Committee to do something about it. He did!

Lectures and tastings at the Wine Trade Club, in 1908 and 1910, were a great success—far too great for comfort. The membership of the Club was growing rapidly and its premises were much too small. Happily, in the winters of 1911, 1912 and 1913, the Vintners' Company gave us the use of their Great Hall for evening classes and lectures, no longer only to Members of the Wine Trade Club, but to all employees in the Wine Trade. It gave technical education a sort of official recognition, and the prestige which it deserved, for the first time in the history of the Wine Trade.

B

The Great Hall of the Vintners was packed, and I had the chance, which I never had before, of showing upon a screen many slides, bought in Paris, showing the different sorts of wine-making grapes and of wine-presses, as well as the more famous wine Châteaux and other items of interest; but nobody came forward to help me and I remained single-handed until 4 August 1914, when I left England, and all who were dearest to me—and all that I would have liked to do—to spend the best part of four years in France and Flanders.

Many of my old students have told me, or written to me, to say how much they had learned from me, how helpful it had been to them, and how grateful they were to me, but I had to live to ninety-two to realize that if it had not been for them, and trying to teach them, I would never have known what I do about Wine!

II. SOUTHAMPTON

IN THE summer of 1894 we were all at Carolles, as we were every year for *les grandes vacances*. When I think of Carolles in those days, I have to pinch myself and make sure that I am awake and not dreaming. There was a farm near the sea at Genets, some two miles short of Avranches, coming from Carolles. It was my father's favourite starting place for a visit to the Mont St. Michel if and when the tide happened to make the crossing across the sands possible in daylight. If we had to make an early start, we had a chance to show our appreciation of the famous Madame Poulard's omelettes: I do not know what they cost, but if we had to wait until after midday to start, we had an early lunch at the farm: home-baked bread, home-made butter, and home-brewed cider *à discretion* which meant as much as you wanted, whether you were discreet or not; then a great omelette with chopped up *fines herbes*, plenty of it; then a leg of lamb and a green salad. And the cost was one franc, ten pence, gold pence before any devaluation, of course, but even then very cheap. Living was incredibly cheap in those days; most people were poor, but not hungry, and anybody with an income like the wages of a London dustman today was quite a rich man!

My brother Jacques had passed brilliantly all sorts of exams and was preparing for St. Cyr, the French military academy: his godfather, the Marquis de Beaufort, a former Zouave Pontifical officer, had made himself responsible for his schooling. I had failed at my *baccalauréat* and all exams; I was only good for *le commerce*, when I left school some eighteen months earlier. The father of one of my father's pupils had given me a trainee job in his office, Rue Duphot, where Prunier came much later. In the evenings, I attended lectures and classes to learn English, Spanish, and Russian, the kind of learning which I liked best. Knowing this, as all the family knew it, my father very wisely suggested that instead of bathing and shrimping at Carolles, it would be better for me to spend a month in England and improve my knowledge of English, and I was, indeed, only too happy to accept his kind offer of one hundred francs for my stay in England. He was by no means a rich man and one hundred francs meant four golden sovereigns—quite some money in those days.

There was at the time a regular cross-Channel service between Southampton and the Channel Islands, Le Havre, Honfleur, and St. Malo, but not Granville. Although I do not know how it was done, I believe that my mother must have written to her sister, Tante Marthe, at St. Servan, St. Malo's twin town, and asked her to find out from the captain or chief officer of the English boat, on her arrival at St. Malo, if he knew anybody in Southampton willing to give a bed to one of her nephews, and feed him for a month; and how much would it cost? She did not waste any time, and soon wrote to my mother that a Captain Coombs, the captain of the St. Malo boat, was willing to have me as a paying guest for a month, for an inclusive sum of one hundred francs! He had two sons just a little younger than I was, and he told Tante Marthe that I would be treated as his third son. And I was. They had a small house in Terminus Terrace, facing the railway line just before it reached the main Southampton Station, which meant getting used to railway whistles and escaping steam, and I had a small room at the back of the house, with a small table and a jug of water in a basin on it, a small chair and a small chest of drawers with three drawers. My belongings were few and did not require more than the two lower drawers, so that I pulled out the top drawer and put it back upside down, and I had its bottom as a desk or writing table. On it I wrote my first letter to the Press. I had seen that day for the first time the French *tricolore* at half mast over Bargate, a sort of town hall or mayor's parlour. I had no idea what it meant, but was told that it was a sign of sympathy upon hearing that the French President, Sadi Carnot, had been assassinated at Lyons. I wrote a letter of thanks to the *Southampton Echo* and signed it André Simon (without the L), and it was in the *Echo* the next evening!

The husband of Tante Marthe, my mother's sister, was Oncle Bricout, organist of the St. Servan pro-cathedral; both of them must have known the old curé for years and Tante Marthe had asked him to give her a short note to the parish priest of the Southampton Catholic church for me. It was an unsealed letter addressed to Canon Scannell, St. Joseph's Church, Southampton, and Tante Marthe gave it to me as she saw me off aboard the Southampton boat. Little did we know that this letter from a curé unknown to me would change the whole of my life. Of course, I read the letter. It just said that I was the nephew of his organist; that all members of my family were good practising Catholics; that I was going to spend a short time in Southampton to improve my knowledge of English; that my stay would be much more pleasant if Canon Scannell could introduce me to Catholic families with children of about my own age.

I soon found where St. Joseph's church was, near the pier, and, like a good boy, I handed my letter to Canon Scannell himself. He did not seem to me to be at all pleased about it. How could he be? He had many Catholic families with lots of children of all ages in his parish, the poor families of Irish dockers who did not speak the Queen's English, but one and no more than one upper middle class family with a number of educated and well behaved children. There were but two rich members—rich for those days! One was Mrs. Dunlop, née Marcel, the daughter of a shipbroker of Le Havre and the widow of George Dunlop, the head of quite an important firm of shipping agents; the other was

her son, Archibald Dunlop, in his thirties, I believe, but
the head of the family business since the untimely death
of his father. They were the only two occupants of the front
bench, on the left or pulpit side, in St. Joseph's church. On
the opposite side the two front benches were occupied by
the Symons family. The father was a white-haired dapper
little man; he was born in Falmouth in 1824, spent all his
working life as a railway engineer, mostly on the construc-
tion of the Great Northern Line, which is why this Cornish-
man's younger children were born at Grantham. The two
youngest, Edith and Gordon, were a little younger than me,
but there were eight more, some a little older than me and
others a great deal older. Only a week or so before I came to
Southampton, the two youngest girls of the Symons family,
Isabel, aged 17, and Edith, aged 15, had come home from
the convent at Angers where they, and their elder sisters
before them, were educated. There were not yet, in England, Catholic girls' schools and convents as there are now.
Isabel was plain, dark, and, I thought, rather silly; she
spoke French with an abominable English accent.

Edith was very different! She was very sweet. Fair of
skin with two tempting little dimples in her cheeks, light
auburn hair, and blue eyes the like of which I had never
seen before, really tender and true; there was affection and
sincerity in them. And she spoke French without the trace
of any accent. Of course, I fell in love with her! I could not
bear the thought of going back to Carolles in a few days.
I did not. I got a job from Archibald Dunlop as office boy,
messenger, dock clerk, or anything else they cared to call
me in the office of George Dunlop and Company. I do not
remember what I was paid; it was certainly not much, but
enough to pay Mrs. Coombs a pound a week for board and
lodging! I returned to Paris in April 1895, at the time of my
father's death; then I had three years of military service to
do before getting a job and marrying, in 1900, my love.

All due to Tante Marthe . . . and Providence!

III. SOUTH AMERICA AND
SOUTH AFRICA

I CANNOT understand how my memory has stored the old plates which are still remarkably good, in fact much better than recent ones. I do not remember what I was given for lunch last Sunday, although I suppose that a good guess would be a joint of some kind, but I do remember quite clearly the first dinner I had when I arrived at Buenos Aires, in November 1907. There was, no doubt, something to begin and something to end with, but what I remember was how excellent were the fish and the bird. I had never tasted the one nor the other before.

The fish was the La Plata Pejerrey or Kingfisher (fish-king in Spanish); beautifully fresh, snow-white, plain baked with melted butter and a squeeze of lime juice. Absolutely delicious. The bird was a batitu from the colder southern part of Argentina, bigger and with a more obvious flavour than a partridge, more like a grouse than any game bird I have ever tasted. After the ship's fare of the previous week, this was a truly memorable occasion. I had noticed during dinner, at a nearby table, people who seemed to be upset about something; I could not understand what they were grumbling about, but I could see that they had a grievance by the way they tackled the head waiter. When they had left the room, and the head waiter came to me, I congratulated him and his chef, and told him how much I had enjoyed my dinner, asking him what had been the trouble with the unhappy people at the nearby table. 'It was the fish they did not like,' said the head waiter. 'Impossible!' I told him, 'it was delicious.' I was quite unable to believe that anybody could find fault with so good a fish. Then the head waiter explained to me that the disgruntled

people were from up-country, miles and miles away towards the Andes where there were no fish, and that, for
them, any fish was a great delicacy which had to come by
train from Buenos Aires, packed in ice, which melted *en
route*, so that they always ate fish which was 'high'. When
they were given fresh fish that evening, they complained
that it had no smell and no real taste. No good at all, by
their standards! It seemed to me incredible, not only that
anybody would eat bad fish, but that they could live to tell
the tale. I always had in mind that stinking fish was
poisonous. But I was wrong, and I little knew, that evening,
that it would not be very long before I would be eating
stinking fish myself.

Our Buenos Aires agent had a friend in Mendoza to
whom he wrote that I would stay a couple of days in
Mendoza, at the foot of the Andes, before going over to
Chile by the mountain railway from Mendoza to Las
Cuevas, the Argentine-Chile frontier. He asked his friend
to arrange for me to visit wineries and vineyards, and the
friend did so with quite unnecessary speed. He announced
my forthcoming visit to one of the largest wine-growers,
who invited him and me to lunch. The mistake made was
in giving the wine-grower too long a notice of my visit; he
had time to wire to Buenos Aires for fish! I knew it as soon
as we entered the house, and I also knew that the poor man
had gone to some real expense, solely to do me honour. How
was I to refuse having any of that stinking fish? I ate it;
it was horrible! I drowned it with glass after glass of red
wine he had made the year before, and that also was
horrible, but much to my surprise and relief, it did not
upset me at all! When I visited Mendoza again, in 1910,
with Jean Calvet and his brother-in-law, Blanchy, on our
way to Chile, we did not announce our visit and we had no
fish. I am still sorry today to have given such a good friend
of mine as Jean Calvet a shock which was as unwise as
unkind. During the long and rather slow climb of the train

from Mendoza to Las Cuevas, Blanchy was resting on his couchette—I forget how many thousands of feet above sea-level, but Jean and I were sharing a bottle of Pommery in the restaurant car; we were the only two. I was going to refill my glass when Jean stopped me and said: 'You had better have no more—you are very red.' 'Am I?' I said stupidly, 'only red? You are black.' He was. He got up at once and took to his couchette until we reached Las Cuevas, and I did the same.

There was no air control whatever in those days either for heat or pressure at high altitudes, but there was a sufficient amount of ice for Champagne to be cold. Of course, nobody wants warm Champagne, but opinions still differ about how cold it should be. Before the war and before my son came to live at Little Hedgecourt, when central heating was put in, my wife and I liked Champagne best when straight from our cold, damp cellar, but most people like it colder. There is no right or wrong degree of coldness; it is a matter of personal opinion—a matter of taste and habit. It is obvious that people used to daily drinks on the rocks, and iced water, will demand very cold Champagne. I remember one occasion when there was no possible argument, and all agreed that the Champagne was too cold. It was at a small dinner party I gave at what was considered at the time the best restaurant in Buenos Aires to celebrate the engagement of a French friend's daughter to the eldest son of Monsieur Danrée, our agent in Montevideo. I had been to the restaurant in the morning to choose fare, wine, table, and flowers, leaving nothing to chance (or so I thought), and to make sure that our little party would be a great success. When we sat down to table, the Sommelier took the bottle of Champagne out of its ice bucket, removed the wire and pulled out the cork without any 'pop'. Then he came to pour some wine in my glass to give me a chance to smell and taste it, but no wine came out of the bottle. It looked very odd. When I looked into the open neck of that Champagne bottle I saw, wedged at the top, what looked like a shining white glass marble. It was a piece of solid ice!

I had a different kind of surprise when, in the early twenties, I registered at the one and only hotel there was at the time in Elizabethville, in the Belgian Congo. I was told that they did stock Pommery Champagne, in fact it was the only Champagne they had, but I must give them at least one hour to get it cold: there was no ice. What they did was to pack the bottle in very wet rags and stand it in a draught, a draught of warm air, of course, and an hour later the rags were quite dry and the wine was quite cold—cold enough to drink. A trick well worth learning and remembering.

I did not stay long in Elizabethville, but was soon back in Bulawayo, where we had a good agent, Blumberg, and where I had an old friend, Tom Meikle. Tom and I were as different as night is from day, but we were very good friends. He was said to be the richest man in Rhodesia, with a chain of first-class hotels (for the time). But whilst he provided only comfort and luxury for the people who asked for it and could pay for it, he had no use for any of it himself. He was not mean, but he was perfectly satisfied with the simplest necessities of life. He told me himself that he did not possess a toothbrush. 'Look at the blacks,' he said, 'they have no toothbrushes, but they have whiter teeth than we have. They use a small piece of soft wood, and so do I.' He was an elderly man when he married a very charming girl, very much younger than he was. The story was at the time that one of his old friends had said to him: 'Tom, don't be an old fool; this young woman is going to spend all your money for you!' 'Yes,' replied Tom quickly, 'that's what I am marrying for!' That story may or may not be true, but I can well imagine Tom not only saying it, but meaning it. He was a lucky man indeed! His wife presented him with three daughters, Joan, Jane and Jean, who were the pride and joy of his old age, and she made the latter part of his life far happier than the rest.

The nineteen twenties were a wonderful decade for gold, diamonds and Champagne in South Africa, which is why I went there every other year, mostly alone, but once with my wife and my daughter Marcelle, and another time with my daughter Jeanne and my son André. Of course, I had a number of friends in every port, but more particularly in Johannesburg, from Affleck, the Secretary of the Rand Club, to Louis Dreyfus, one of the pillars of the Long Bar, and most of the barmaids who were good looking on the whole, and all of whom were intelligent, well dressed and well informed.

The only unfortunate incident I remember during my visits to South Africa happened in Durban. There were a few French wool-burgers there, all of them from Reims, but what was more curious was that there was, at the time, a French Catholic Bishop who was a native of Reims. I asked him to dine at my hotel with the wool-burgers and he was delighted at the prospect of an all-Reims meeting, as well as a glass of Champagne. On the appointed day we were all waiting for him when a telephone message came through to say that the bishop was unable to come and would I see him in the morning. We were all very disappointed, and the next day I called to know what had happened. The poor bishop was furious. He had been just ready to leave when the telephone bell rang. Had he taken up the receiver all would have been well, but his assistant took it, and heard from a young fusspot in charge of the wireless station that the news had just come through of the Pope's death. 'My lord,' cried the man, 'our Holy Father is dead. We must hold a service for the repose of his soul.' And the poor bishop lost the one and only chance he had ever had, so far as I know, to drink Champagne and talk with men from his homeland!

During the twenties and thirties, keener competition between shipping companies for as great a share as possible of the passenger traffic was responsible for more being done for the comfort and entertainment of passengers; such as bathrooms, some even attached to de luxe cabins. Ships also had bands. Before 1910, there was only one bath in the sick bay, and nothing was done for the entertainment of passengers—which did not mean that they had a dull time, however. They entertained themselves; there was always somebody who could play the cornet or accordion, or who could sing, or get up charades or new games. I remember a man offering a bottle of Champagne to any lady who could sit on her hair; only three did; they were rather short, and their hair, when let down, went past that part of their anatomy which nature has well padded for comfort when sitting. The taller women had no longer hair than the small ones, and no chance at all!

When I came home from Chile, early in 1908, I had to travel from Valparaiso to Callao by cargo boat, and forget about gastronomy—but it was worth it: I would never have seen otherwise a fleet of three-masted barques leaving Iquique for Dunkirk, full of nitrates—a truly memorable sight!

Another memorable sight, but a horrible one, on that home-bound trip, was a cock-fight in Martinique. An old veteran fighting cock, who had lost one eye in a previous fight, was put in the pit with a young cockerel, backed to win by almost everybody. The old cock ran as fast as he could, round and round the pit, with the young one running after him, giving the poor old cock bird stabs with his spurs, but all of a sudden the half blind veteran flew up and stuck his spur right into the head of the young cock, who fell down dead.

IV. FIRST AVIATION WEEK, 1909

IN 1908, when the London Wine Trade Club was founded, I had suggested that its first President should be my friend A. S. Gardiner, the Editor of the *Wine and Spirits Review*. He had been elected President and I had been elected Vice-President both for one year. In 1909 I became the President for one year, and in 1910 I was elected sole Trustee 'in perpetuity'. None of us, in the Wine Trade, at that time ever dreamt that the Wine Trade Club would cease to exist long before its Trustee, and that most of the Wine Trade as we knew it would be swallowed up by Brewers, Distillers and financial groups in mergers and such-like modern devices. But, in 1909, I was also Chairman of the Wine Trade Club Education Committee, and I had promised the Members to take a party of them each year to one of the principal wine-producing districts of Europe at vintage time as it would give them a chance to see the vineyards, and how wine was made, as well as tasting wines of past vintages in the cellars of local wine-growers and wine-shippers. The programme gave Champagne in 1909, Bordeaux in 1910 and Rhineland Moselle in 1911. The time was to be mid-September or late September according to vintage time. However when I heard that there was to be the first ever Aviation Show, the Première Semaine d'Aviation at Bétheny, near Reims during the last week of August 1909, I decided that my friends and myself would have a great many other occasions to see grapes being picked and pressed but never again to be present at what might be called the most memorable flying start. So it was decided that the first Education Committee visit to vineyards would be the last week in August.

Of course, there were people from many parts of the world who wanted to be there also, and when the time came there was not a bed to be had for love or money in or near Reims. I believe that there were special trains which brought crowds from Paris each morning and took them back at night. But my little group of thirteen members of the Wine Trade Club and myself had no difficulty whatever.

Melchior, Marquis De Polignac, twenty-seven years old then, and the eldest grandson of the original Veuve Pommery, was not only the President of the Semaine d'Aviation Committee, but he had worked tooth and nail day and night to make it the success that it proved to be. We had been friends for years and my father and his father had been friends ever since they had been comrades in arms during the war of 1870/71. Thanks to him, our party was given one of the Pommery firm's garages and the *vendangeur*'s beds, bedsteads stored for the people who come at vintage time, like hop-pickers in Kent, to help in the picking of the grapes. There was a tap for washing, and a hose for hosing each other in the morning—the only fairly cool time of the day. During a week of tropical August heat, Melchior de Polignac had also given us Press tickets and seats for the show and provided transport to take us to Bétheny each morning and back to Reims in time for lunch. There was much excitement and heated arguments about monoplanes and bi-planes. As Blériot had crossed the Channel in July in his monoplane, the double deckers were not the favourites.

The world records for height, distance and speed were smashed at Bétheny by Latham with the dizzy height of 58 metres, the distance by Farman with 190 kilometres and for speed by Paulhan with 131 kilometres in two hours 43 minutes and $24\frac{4}{5}$ seconds!

Five of our mornings were given to Bétheny and flying, but the rest of the day to education (partly), and meals and jollification (mostly). We visited vineyards of course, as well as cellars during working hours in Reims, Epernay, Ay and Avize, but the generosity of our hosts was beyond the dreams of both gourmets and gourmands.

For our first lunch we were the guests of Charles Heidsieck on 27 August 1909, a very hot day, really too hot for me, much as I love sunshine; my friends felt the heat even more than I did, more particularly the older ones, Roland Lane, the wine buyer of Booth Distillery and Arthur Spencer, the Walter Symons of Mark Lane. When we arrived sweating and panting just after 1 o'clock, rather late by French standards, we went straight down the deep *crayères*, the old Roman chalk pits which serve as cellars, and there was a beautifully laid table on trestles with such tempting plain carafes full of pale gold wine waiting for us. No speeches, no cocktails; we sat down anywhere we liked. Charles Heidsieck *père* asked me to sit next to him; some of his sons and senior members of his firm each took a member of our party in charge, but the first thing that was given to us was not Champagne but a rug to put over our knees, and then came a black woollen shawl for our shoulders. The temperature was just about 10° Centigrade or 50° Fahrenheit, a wonderful rest for us all but a real danger of catching a bad cold, after coming down from some 90° above ground. The *vin blanc en carafe* on the table was our first drink of the day and absolute nectar. We had taken for granted, or at any rate I had, that it was a *vin ordinaire pour la soif*; but it was very far from *ordinaire*. It was a truly delicious Cramant 1900 still *blanc de blancs*, the best still Champagne I could remember having drunk when I lived in Reims and had lunch *chez* Monsieur Puisard, Pommery's Steward for the Côte des Blancs Vineyard. Of course, none of my party had ever tasted a still Champagne and they were amazed. It was lesson No. 1 of the Education Committee on tour. *Grand succès*. The food, of course, was cold and excellent, the only wine served with the meal was Charles Heidsieck 1900, at cellar temperature, of course, just right, and we all enjoyed this lunch enormously. We were most reluctant when the time came to go. We had asked a Spanish firm who made Champagne corks, near the Porte de Paris, to show our party how Champagne corks were cut out of the cork bark and made to the size and shape any client asked for. Four cabs had been ordered to wait for us outside Charles Heidsieck's office, take us to the Porte de Paris, wait for us and bring us back to our garage home.

When we emerged from the cold *crayères* into the terrific heat of that August day we were hardly able to goose-step our way to the cabs only a short way away. We were so wobbly—quite sober, of course—that we were glad to have a seat in a cab to sit down, and, as far as I was concerned, go to sleep. I never saw, but I can so well visualize how those four cabs looked in single file, like a funeral procession having lost the hearse. I am sorry to say that I cannot remember if and when we arrived at the Spanish cork firm. I suppose that we must have done so, but I am afraid that none of us were in the right mood to take an intelligent interest in Champagne corks.

The next day was another sunny day, but whether there was a little breeze or because we were becoming acclimatized to high temperatures, we did not find the heat nearly as much as we had the day before.

We were the guests for lunch, on that day, of Raoul de Bary who owned at the time the Veuve George Goulet brand of Champagne. He gave us a superb meal in his house on Boulevard Lundy, Champagne of different vintages and a surprise, which was almost a shock: a large glass of Vintage Port at the end of the meal. The fourteen of us were in the Wine Trade and knew that Brown Gore and Welch were the London agents of George Goulet as well as Offley Forrester, so we were not surprised to find that Raoul de Bary had some Offley's Vintage Port, but we were surprised that he had given it to us on such a hot day. This brings back to my memory 'Baby' Gore, who was no baby at all but the senior partner of Brown Gore and Welch. I knew him very well. He was a little man but a great tennis player, one of the stars of Wimbledon when tennis was a game and not hard hitting as it is now. Although I never either heard him say so himself, or deny it, tennis players in those days were told that the little wonder affectionately known as Baby Gore always drank half a bottle of George Goulet before stepping on the court. Whether it was really so or not, and, if true, whether it was good or not for his tennis, I cannot say, but it was not bad publicity for George Goulet.

That evening we were the guests of Champagne St. Marceaux, in Reims. The fare was wonderful and so were the wines, a Blanc de Blancs 1905 as an apéritif; an Avize 1892 with the fish course and then a Carte d'Or 1884, a pre-phylloxera, twenty-five-year-old wine, the oldest Champagne my 'students' had ever tasted, and an amazingly fresh wine for its age—although, naturally, not violently sparkling. To finish with a Carte d'Or 1898, more lively but mature withal. A real treat indeed!

The next day, 29 August, we were the guests of Pommery, which I called my firm in those days, and the meal was very good but very simple, by Reims standards, with only one wine, Pommery 1900, by request. I knew that we were to dine that evening as the guests of G. H. Mumm Champagne, who were likely to give us a *festin*, a great deal to eat and all of the very best, as well as quite a number of very fine wines, and this is exactly what they did; the fare was superb and the wines a 1906 Cramant Blanc de Blancs to begin with, a Cordon Rouge 1898 with the fish course, a really remarkable 1900 Bouzy Rouge with the first course of meat; this was the first time my 'students' had tasted a still red Champagne, and they thoroughly approved of it. We came back to orthodox Champagne with Magnums of 1892 with the next four or five courses, and ended with an old Boa Vista Vintage Port. How well we all slept that night!

c

The next day, 30 August, we went over the Montagne de
Reims to Ay where we visited the Bollinger cellars and
enjoyed some sparkling refreshment before crossing the
Marne and being the guests of Moët et Chandon for lunch.
The lunch was meant to be simple, by request, but it was
quite delicious. There were only two wines after the usual
Blanc de Blancs opening wine, a blend of Cramant and
Le Mesnil wines both of the 1893 vintage, the oldest still
Champagne we had tasted. The Cuvée was quite a nice
wine, but, of course, not in the same class as the wine
which followed—the Cuvée 36 of 1889. I had often said
and I most sincerely meant it that the Pommery CBA 1889
Cuvée was the finest Champagne bar none, but from August
1909 to this day I have said 'bar one'. The Cuvée 36 was
the challenge Champagne *in excelsis*, the like of which the
younger generations have never seen and can never see
again. Of course, there has been much good and very good
Champagne made during the past eighty years, and there
is some very good Champagne made today. I still drink
Champagne which I greatly enjoy, but I still treasure the
memory of those true 1889 Cuvées as something that was
exceptional.

That evening we dined at Avize as the guests of Messrs
Giesler who gave us wines which neither I nor any of my
'students' ever tasted before or since. Needless to say the
fare was both plentiful and excellent, but by now we took it
for granted that it would be so. We were given a very old
Sherry to begin with; quite a surprise, of course, and a very
pleasant one. A very nice Avize 1899 was served with the
fish course, then a Château Léoville 1887 with the first
meat course: that was another surprise but I believe that
most of us were rather sorry not to have a Bouzy Rouge
rather than the Claret. We did not have to wait long for
the Bouzy Rouge. It came next, and incredible as it may
appear, its vintage was 1865! Of course, it must have been
a better wine when twenty years younger, but it was by

no means too old; there was no trace whatever of acetic acid; it had lost some colour but still had great charm. We were brought back to earth and the joy of youth with an Avize 1904 followed by a special Cuvée 1899 and an Avize from 1893, the only Blanc de Blancs wine of all those we had tasted that had both more body and colour than the rest. And as we had been given Sherry to begin with for the first time, we were given an 1830 Cognac Grande Fine Champagne for the first time to finish with.

The next day, 31 August, we had the most spectacular meal of our trip when we were the guests of Heidsieck Dry Monopole Champagne for lunch at the Moulin de Verzenay, perched on a spur of the Montagne de Reims, overlooking thousands of acres of vines from the main Reims to Châlons-sur-Marne road up the hills as far as and beyond the villages below the woodlands which cover the top of the Montagne. There is but one large, long room in the Moulin, three of its sides all glass, so that one can enjoy the truly magnificent panorama. Year after year, day after day, visitors from all parts of the world have come to this unique observatory and admired the view that we admired, but there was on this last day of August 1909 another view which, I believe, had never been seen before and was never seen again. Upon a long refectory table almost as long as the room, there stood twenty-four Magnums of Dry Monopole 1892, one Magnum for each of the twenty-four men who sat down to lunch, fourteen of us and ten others; some of them members of the firm, others their guests. The fare was cold and very good and nobody was in a hurry. As far as I could tell the only cheating, if cheating it may be called, was Otto Winterschlaøden of Middlesbrough, the youngest member of the party, helping Roland Lane, the oldest of us, who found a Magnum rather more than he could drink.

We left Reims at the crack of dawn on 2 September 1909 by the Calais-Basle train for Calais—Dover and London, but the night before we gave a banquet to our kind hosts just to show them that we could give as well as take and we made sure they would not go home hungry! I still have the menu of this banquet. I cannot see it, but when I had it read to me, I could not help wondering whether we really ate it all; I believe we did. Here it is:

Melon
Consommé Madrilène
Turbotin braisé au Champagne
Petites Timbales de Volaille Régence
Selle d'Agneau Bouquetière
Jambon de Parme en Bellevue
Caneton de Rouen à la Presse
Salade
Demoiselles de Caen à la Nage
Rocher d'Aviation
Laitances et Champignons sur Toast
Corbeille de Fruits
Friandises
Dessert.

There was no wine list; Champagne was the only wine and one could call for any brand of the firms who had been our hosts during our visit; they were all there. It was a truly festive occasion and a great success. I asked Charles Heidsieck to sit next to me, as he had asked me to sit next to him at our first meal, otherwise all sat where they liked and with whom they liked.

Many weeks later, at about midday, Arthur Spencer rang me up and asked me to come to his office, next but one to my own at 24 Mark Lane, adding he had a surprise for me. I went and Arthur's 'staff', Charles, brought a bottle of Pommery which was opened forthwith. But that was no surprise. The surprise was a very nice silver cigarette box with the date of the Reims aviation week and the names of members of the party in alphabetical order.

I thanked them, of course, but I could not help saying that I thought they knew that I never smoked cigarettes. 'Of course, we know that perfectly well, but we also know that your wife smokes cigarettes, and we want you to give her this box as a token of our gratitude to her for letting you come to Reims with us. It did make all the difference.' There are no longer any cigarettes in that box, but it is still and it will be to the end one of my more cherished possessions.

P.S. Thanks to the kind thought of Joseph Dargent, my daughter Jeanne and I were the guests of the C.I.V.C. or Comité Interprofessionnel du Vin de Champagne, during the first week of July 1967, the year before my old eyes failed me. It gave me great joy to see once more, and for the last time, the cathedral of Reims and the old church of St. Rémi, the tomb of Dom Pérignon at Hautvillers, and the vineyards and villages of Champagne which I had known and loved all my grown-up life! We were hospitably entertained by members of the present-day generation of the Champagne trade but there were no more than two of real age with whom to talk about olden days: Princesse Henri de Polignac and Joseph Krug.

Diane de Polignac was a school girl when I first came to Reims; I do not remember what her face was like, but only her back with two lengths of plaited red hair. She is now nearly eighty and crippled by arthritis, the only grand-daughter of the original Veuve Pommery, and the only surviving child of Guy de Polignac, my father's friend. She married the Prince Henri de Polignac, so did not change her name. Prince Henri was wounded at Perthes-les-Hurlus, on 28 February 1915, when my brother Roger was killed, and he was killed at the Chemin des Dames, in 1917, the day my brother Jacques was wounded. His eldest son, Prince Guy de Polignac, is now at the head of the family business. There cannot be many people today, if any, who have known Diane as long as I have—some seventy years!

We were the guests of Jean and Madame Couvreur, in Reims, the evening before we left for London. I did not know Jean, now the head of the G. H. Mumm Champagne firm, but I used to know, many years ago, both his father and his uncle who owned Duminy. I was very glad and rather surprised to hear from Jean Couvreur that my old friend Joseph Krug, now ninety-eight years old, was still alive. Jean Couvreur rang up Joseph Krug's grandson, a friend of his, and asked him whether we could see his grandfather the next morning, before leaving Reims. The grandson said he could not tell; his grandfather had good days and bad days and if he had a good day, he would let us know and call for us, which he did. Joseph Krug was wonderful when we called at 11 o'clock. We had a bottle of Krug 1953 together. He stood up erect, remembered names and dates. I was astounded then, and greatly shocked when some two weeks later I learnt that he had died in his sleep.

V. IN THE WITNESS BOX

ONCE upon a time, a long, long time ago, when I first came to England, there were two bad men in London: one was an Englishman and the other a Frenchman: birds of a feather, they worked together. The Englishman was a banqueting wine waiter, that is a part-time waiter called in on nights when extra staff happened to be wanted for large parties. The Frenchman was a wine 'expert'. They had a cellar under one of the arches below the Adelphi: the Englishman collected empty Champagne bottles and corks, brought them to his partner who filled the bottles with a cheap, sweetish white wine, pumped a dash of gas in it, corked the bottle, wired it, and dressed it with a little gold or silver paper to match the rest of the foil. The Englishman had a wonderful frock coat with six leather inside pockets, three left and three right, and he would go to Hurst Park and other race meetings near London, with a stock of fake Champagne in a cart; he would mix with the crowd and offer 'first-class Champagne' at 5s. per bottle. The price was tempting and out of the six pockets of his frock coat came the bottles of Champagne asked for, just as a conjuror produces a live rabbit out of a top-hat. One Saturday afternoon, at Hurst Park, a clerk from the offices of Messrs. Moët et Chandon's London agents had a win and called for a bottle of his firm's wine: the bottle that was handed to him looked quite right to him, but he happened to look at the cork as it came out with remarkable promptness, and there was no possible doubt about the lettering burnt on the side of the cork: it was POMMERY and not MOËT. This is how the man with the six-pocket frock coat was arrested and charged by the London agents of Moët

and Pommery. Robert Billings, for Moët, and I for Pommery, gave evidence in Court, and we agreed that it was
possible, even probable, that both firms had bought corks
from the same Spanish cork merchants, but that it was
quite impossible for Moët to use Pommery corks, as each
firm did its own branding of the corks in its cellars; and
between the Moët cellars at Epernay, and the Pommery
cellars at Reims, there were some miles of hills, woods and
vineyards. Eventually the man was found guilty, and fined
some ridiculous sum—I forget exactly what it was, but I
know that he paid it at once and went home.

Some time after, not very long, I had a visit from the
police at Mark Lane, and I was informed that the rogue was
at his old game again. 'Good luck to him', I said, much to
the officer's surprise, adding that it had cost us about £200
to get him convicted a first time, and we were not prepared
to spend any more money on legal proceedings. So that
time, he was caught again, charged by the Public Prosecutor
and sent to prison without the option of a fine. I thought
it would be the last that I would hear of him; but I was
wrong. The fellow had a wife, and she came to my office,
asking, in a very loud and querulous voice, what we were
going to do for her whilst her 'good man' was in jug! His
'partner' had vanished and could not help her. Nor could we.

The next time I was in the witness box, the case had a far
more satisfactory ending. The traveller of a City firm who
sold a great deal of the cheaper types of wine in the London
East End had called upon one of his regular customers to be
told that he, the traveller, need not call any more for orders
as his wines were too dear. The traveller swore that there
were no cheaper wines than those sold by his firm, and
when he was given what his former customer sold as wine,
he spat it out and said in the presence of all in the room
'This is not wine; it is poison!' The publican brought an
action for slander, demanding damages from the traveller's
firm. The head of the firm accused of slander came to see

me and asked me to taste a sample of the 'poison' wine, and tell him whether he had better settle the matter out of court, or go to court with a fair chance of winning. There was no need to taste the stuff; its stink was enough. I advised going to Court, and promised to give evidence—which I did. When in the witness box I was given a full glass and asked to say what the wine was. I tasted it and said that it was a cheap but fair enough wine, probably from Algeria. I was then given another full glass and asked the same question. The moment the glass came near my nose I knew what it was and did not taste it. 'This', I said, 'I can swear is not wine, but I cannot tell you what it is. You had better ask a drain inspector.' The prosecution lost the case and had to pay all costs, but that was not all: the defence made the prosecuting publican admit that he did not buy the stuff; he made it on the premises!

Shortly after the case, the man was prosecuted by either the Public Prosecutor or the Wine and Spirit Association, and convicted of fraud. He probably lost his licence, but this I cannot remember.

I never felt nervous in the witness box, nor rattled by any questions of the lawyers, but once only, at the Mansion House, I was very unhappy about being there. It was nobody's fault but my own. I was the one and only witness for the defence of a wine-merchant whom I did not know, but there were lots of witnesses for the prosecution, most of whom I did know as the sons or grandsons of old friends of mine. There had not been any Port shipped to England after 1940 during the war years, so that Port was now in short supply, and there had been cases of wine being sold as Port which had no right to the name. The Port Wine Shippers Association had quite rightly prosecuted the wrong-doers with the necessary publicity to stop the rot. It stopped the rot, but it did not stop the prosecutions and the Wine Trade journals went on giving the names of all sorts of hitherto quite unknown wine-merchants who had been prosecuted and found guilty. They always were. There always were witnesses for the prosecution, Port shippers who swore that the wine in the case was not genuine Port, but there never was a single witness for the defence. It had nothing to do with me, I know, but somehow or other I could not help feeling sorry for the victims of the Port Wine Shippers Association's zeal, which seemed to me unnecessarily harsh. I was in that mood when I happened to meet a lawyer who told me that he had been asked by a wine-merchant whom he had every reason to believe was a most honourable and honest man, to act for him; the unfortunate wine-merchant was being prosecuted and was, of course, bound to be convicted, as he could not hope to get any witness for the defence. Whether I was stupid or merely quixotic, I cannot now say, but I said that I would stand in the witness box for him. This I did after tasting his wine, which was, I considered, quite acceptable as Port. All I said in the witness box was that I could not swear that the wine was Oporto Port, nor could I swear that it was not, but if I had been given it at the Savoy or Dorchester, I would have accepted it, and drunk it, just as all the witnesses for the prosecution would have done, I was sure. They certainly would not have prosecuted the Savoy or the Dorchester. For the first time, the accused wine-merchant was not fined: the case was dismissed by the Lord Mayor, and so far as I know, there has not been another prosecution by the Port Wine Shippers Association since this. But I was very unpopular at the time. My friends said that I was so old that I had lost my taste; those who were not my friends said that I was so poor that I had been paid. All were wrong.

The last time I was in the witness box was at the time of the Spanish Champagne case, as happy an occasion as the Port case had been unhappy. I was fortunate in being asked by the Q.C. for the defence, a question with the easiest possible of answers: 'Is there any difference', I was asked, 'between Spanish Champagne and Spanish Chablis or Spanish Sauternes, accepted on most wine lists in England?' 'Yes,' I said 'there is a difference. Chablis is a small market town; Sauternes is a small village. When their names were taken to help to sell Spanish white wines, there may have been half a dozen people in Chablis, but none at all in Sauternes, with the money to pay their fares to London, and no more. But Champagne is not a small market town; it is not a small village; it is much bigger than Yorkshire, with large cities and many firms who have great stocks of fine wine, and the means to be here today asking for justice, asking that their most valuable asset, their name, be not taken from them, as the names of poor Chablis and Sauternes were taken. That is the difference.'

And since then Champagne has had its name protected by the law of England, as Port has had its name protected since 1916.

Bath stone is soft stone in the eyes of an Aberdonian, and not all Bath houses are built of Bath stone. One of them, which was built in the summer of 1939, is built on mud: it stands on foundations which were driven deep down into the mud by a great weight hauled up by a crane and dropped, time after time, day after day. The noise was a nuisance, of course, for the people next door, who happened to be wine-merchants with a large stock of Vintage Port in their cellars.

The vibrations caused by the incessant pile-driving disturbed the sediment of the Port to such an extent that the wine was 'out of condition' and unsaleable. The wine-merchants asked for damages and they were offered a trifling sum which they indignantly refused to accept. They asked me to come to Bath, look at their wines and assess the damage they had suffered. I did so and named the figure which I considered to be fair compensation. Then came the war. I heard no more and I had forgotten all about it when I received another request to come to Bath on a certain day, some fairly long time ahead, and give evidence on behalf of the wine-merchants, who had failed to obtain any redress from the builders, and were suing them for damages. I wrote back and said that I had better come down to Bath at once and have another look at their wines; which I did. I found that their Vintage Port, having had time to recover from its shaking, was no worse than before: I even thought that it was all the better for it. My original figure could no longer be justified. Moreover, there was no more Port reaching England, and the duty on Port, which was 8s. per gallon in 1939, had been raised to 12s. per gallon, in 1940, and to 16s. in 1941: the next year it was put up to 28s. which meant that these merchants' stock had become a great deal more valuable. I told them that in a court of law the defendants' Counsel would have no difficulty in cross-examining me to make me agree that the pile-driving of their clients had given the complaining wine-merchants an unhoped-for chance of selling their Port not only more readily but also much more profitably. My advice to them was to accept whatever sum the builders were offering to pay, and not to waste any money on legal proceedings. Which is what they did.

VI. PRE-PHYLLOXERA WINES

THERE cannot be many, if any, people alive today who have enjoyed, as I have, most of the great pre-phylloxera wines when they were (and I was) in their prime.

Were pre-phylloxera wines better than today's wines? This is a question which I have often been asked, but all I could say without any hesitation was that they were considerably cheaper, and that if the wines of the good vintages were better, the wines of bad vintages were certainly worse before the phylloxera. Thanks to science, there are no more undrinkable wines made, even when the sun fails to ripen the grapes and when they are picked un-ripe and mouldy, as some were in the Médoc in 1963. Chemistry and technology work marvels, not to say miracles, quite unheard of before the phylloxera. All but one of the *Grands crus* of the Gironde have given their Château bottling to the wines of 1963 which would have been written off as a dead loss in 1863!

It is usually easy enough to tell which is the worse of two bad wines, but it is extremely difficult to tell which is the better of two good wines. It is possible, of course, to know how much alcohol and other matters there are in a wine, but it has little to do with the wine's quality. The value of a gold ornament can be assessed by its gold carats, but the quality of wine is a matter of personal opinion—which is liable to vary with your palate, your mood, the temperature of the room, and other such factors. Which is why it is so difficult to compare two or more fine wines and decide which is the best!

Of course, all the *Grands Crus* of the Médoc of 1864, 1875 and all the pre-phylloxera good years were really great wines, perfectly balanced, with great charm, and so were the great Vintage Ports from 1847 to 1868, as well as the wines of Burgundy, Champagne, the Rhine and Moselle, but it would be unfair and untrue to forget how good were the *Grands Crus* of the Médoc of 1899 and 1900, the 1908 and 1912 Vintage Ports, and many more post-phylloxera wines. Were the wines of the older generations better, and if so, how much better, is very difficult or impossible to say. How many pre-phylloxera wines which I remember, for instance, could be compared to the Cheval Blanc 1921, a freak wine I know—unlike any Claret I ever drank, but a great wine for a time.

Quality in wine is not a matter of fact, but a matter of sensual impact: the brain gives the verdict after hearing from the three senses of sight, smell and taste, which is why difference in the quality of pre- and post-phylloxera wines must remain a matter of personal opinion. There is, however, a difference between them which is a matter of fact. The pre-phylloxera wines had a much longer lease of life, which is not surprising since they were made from the grapes of very old vines, that is young shoots of almost ageless vines, whereas, since the phylloxera, the grafted vines have to be replanted every twenty or twenty-five years.

As Cellarer of the Saintsbury Club for the first thirty years of its existence, I was able to buy and nurse twelve bottles of Château Lafite 1870 to be served at one of our Dinners, in 1950 when my old friend Ian Campbell, who was born in 1870, and the Claret would both be eighty. Ian was more sparkling than the wine, but the Lafite had more colour and was a real joy: old, of course, but by no means too old; without any trace of acetic acid or decay! How different from the Cheval Blanc 1921 which was 'peeping over'; that is, beginning to go downhill at twenty!

When I returned to my old Mark Lane office, in 1919, after the war, we still had four Magnums of Cockburn 1847. They soon went the way all good wines are made to go! Not because they were getting old; they were not, but because they were so wonderfully delicious: they were seventy-two years young, and might have been still fit to drink at 100! The 1927 Vintage Ports were very fine for many years but not for forty! As to the post-war Vintage Ports, who would care to lay any down for twenty years? Not me: I am ninety-two!

I have among my old Wine Trade papers the wine-list of a London wine-merchant which is dated 1860: there are four brands of Champagne listed: Moët et Chandon, G. H. Mumm, Perrier Jouet, and Giesler, and the vintage is the same for the four: 1846! Today most people would consider a 1953 Champagne much too old. If we want to know how young a white wine, still or sparkling, is now considered fit to sell and to drink, we must go to the Rhineland! Hocks and Moselles, sweeter and dearer than they ever were, are now sold when one year old: they probably think that I am too old, but do not say so; I think that they are too young, and I do say so.

VII. WORLD WAR I

I LEFT London on 3 August 1914 for Paris, in the morning—in spite of André, my eldest boy, begging me not to go until the evening after his birthday tea party; he was eight years old on that day. On 4 August, I was at Vincennes and joined the queue of ex-gunners of the 13th Artillery Regiment who had already flocked from all parts of France to report. If the truth be known, I was not there because of a burning desire to fight and die for my country, but because I was an incorrigible optimist and felt quite certain that I would be sent home at once. I had taken a return ticket at Victoria available for one month, and I had the return half safely in my wallet: I have it still! Not in my wallet, but with the Military Medal and other war souvenirs. Not only because of my age (I was nearly forty) but because of my unique three years of service *militaire*, I had never seen, let alone fired a gun. I could not possibly be of any use to the 13th Artillery Regiment. When my turn came to be at the recruiting sergeant's desk, I knew that he would tell me to get away and go home. But he did nothing of the sort. He asked me what was my job and I did not like to say that I had anything to do with wine, as he might have put me in charge of the canteen, so I said that I was an *Homme de lettres*—a man of letters. 'Good', said the recruiting sergeant right away and added 'I have a job for you'. He took a green card that was on his desk; it had rubber stamps and signatures on it, so that all he had to do was to write my name on it and give it to me, saying 'this is an official *laissez-passer* which you must be very careful not to lose. They will let you go out and come in at any time if you show it at the barrack gates; you will go to the Post Office every day and they will give you all the letters for those who serve in the Regiment. Get out. Who is next?' I got out and it took me some time to realize that I had never before been more truly a man of letters than I was now as regimental postman! Any doubting Thomas is welcome to see that green card, which has been at rest during the past fifty years with the return half of my London–Paris ticket.

I knew that it would be useless to argue with the recruiting sergeant, but the officer who had signed my green card had *capitaine* after his name, and I hoped that he might be more understanding. I managed to get somebody who could read what his name was and somebody else who showed me where his office was. I was no longer the super-optimist I had been forty-eight hours earlier, and I had no intention of asking this captain to send me home. All I proposed to ask him was to tell me how I could become an interpreter attached to one of the units of the British Expeditionary Force instead of being a Vincennes army postman. He asked me for my *Livret Militaire* and I handed it to him. It is a sort of identity card which all Frenchmen are given after their *service militaire* with their name, date and place of birth and qualifications. The captain looked at the qualifications, gave me back my *livret* and told me to get on and not to tell him that I could speak English when all there was in my book was that I could read, write and swim. Nothing about English. I ought to have told him that my *Livret Militaire* was not up to date, but I had been told to get out in such a way that I got out.

I started to think how best I could prove to the captain that I was not a liar! I came to the conclusion that I would write two very short books on the same subject, one in English and one in French, which would make it abundantly clear that I knew both languages. What would be a good subject to choose, I asked myself. I ruled out Champagne as wartime is not the best Champagne time, and when I

D

discovered that the chapel in one of the barracks courts must have ceased to be used as a chapel for many years, since it was now a library, with shelf upon shelf of bound copies of the *Revue d'Artillerie* and *Revue du Génie*, I decided to write, in English, and to publish in England, a book about General Joffre, the head of the French, and I would also write in French all about Marshal French, a book that would be published in Paris at the same time. I knew from my *service militaire* days that all artillery officers had their mutations, promotions, citations, and decorations duly recorded and I was sure that the same was done for the sappers (Joffre was a sapper, not a gunner) in the *Revue du Génie*. Strange as it certainly is *Génie* means genius in ordinary French, but Engineers in military French. So it was just a matter of patience, looking through the official part of the *Revue du Génie* to find where and when General Joffre had risen from *sous-lieutenant* to Generalissimo, where he had been serving, and what decorations he had been given. I added, of course, a few words of praise or commentary here and there, just as a few sprigs of parsley will decorate a dish of fish.

It was published at one shilling by Simpkin Marshall, with two photographs of the general which were found in London. The book in French was much simpler. One of the London magazines published a number devoted entirely to Marshal French; it was sent to me, and I translated most of it, and added the usual sprigs of parsley, and it was published in Paris by Lethielleux, rue Cassette, paper backed, to be bought for fifty centimes, or fivepence. Lethielleux published at the same time a translation, in French, of my General Joffre, also at fifty centimes or fivepence.

When I went to see the captain with my little books, I felt quite sure that victory was round the corner. He would now know that I did not lie and maybe beg my pardon. He did nothing of the sort. He flew into a violent rage, and shouted that I must be mad. How did I dare publish books about anything at all without leave to do so, and the censor's permit. But to write about my chiefs was a clear case for prison during the duration of the war for me. He did not mind that, but he was afraid of being in trouble himself for aiding and abetting my crime. 'I would send you to hell if I knew how to do it', he added after sitting at his desk for a while, with his head in both hands, obviously wondering what he should do. It must have been then that he remembered having received an official circular from the French War Office asking that soldiers who could be spared and who knew English well should be sent to Le Havre, to the Headquarters of a new military organization known as *La Mission*—whose mission it was to appoint interpreters asked for by units of the British Expeditionary Force. So, as he did not have the necessary transport to send me to hell, he sent me instead to Le Havre to be an interpreter, which was all I had been asking for! The books had done the trick after all! Today, so much older and maybe a little wiser, it seems to me incredible that I once had the impudence to publish a book with a photo of Joffre on the cover with the caption 'General Joffre by a French gunner'. I wonder if there was at any time and in any army another private soldier who put down in print, in wartime, what he thought of the Commander in Chief?

I was posted to the Headquarters of the R.A.S.C. of the 50th (Northumbrian) Division as they landed at Le Havre, to be sent straight to Ypres just after the first German gas attack. I was given a batman who was a Durham pitman before the war, but I soon became used to his voice and ways. He was very good to me and my horse; we never missed, nor wanted for anything, but others sometimes did. I remember putting on my socks one day, and seeing a clear LIBBY on the tab; Libby was our M.O. at the time. 'Arthur,' I called, 'you have given me the Doctor's socks.' 'Quite right, Sir,' said Arthur, 'he would have given them to you himself if he had seen your socks; nothing but holes. Don't worry, Sir, he has lots more!'

When winter came, the 50th Division was stuck in the mud of Flanders, west of Ypres, near Poperinghe, and it looked to me that we might be there for a very long time. Of course, I knew absolutely nothing of the war, how and why it ever started, still less how it was proceeding, but I had all the same built up a picture in my mind, which seemed to me to be reasonable and likely to be near enough to the truth. I believed that the Germans knew that France was quite unprepared for war, but that they did not know that Britain would back France. They had been confident of a lightning victory on the western front before turning, with all their might, to the Russian menace. When their confidence had been badly shaken, or shattered at the Battle of the Marne, they must have realized that the war would be much longer than they had anticipated; it meant making more armaments and munitions, as it did also for France and Britain. Which was why troops on both sides would have to stay put during the winter of 1915, just holding their ground, with an occasional shell or two at midday and midnight to let each other know that they were not asleep, whilst day and night, seven days each week, work was going on at home making guns, shells, and all that was required for hell on earth in the spring. There had been talk at the men's table that some chosen British officers and men might be sent in the spring by ship to Archangel to train and help the Russians, our Allies then. As I was desperately anxious to have something to do, it gave me the idea of writing to my wife asking her to look for any book about Russian that she might find among my books. She found a Russian grammar and a Russian-French dictionary, which she sent to me. It was all I wanted to put together a very elementary booklet likely to help British officers and men to ask for what they wanted in Russian. I sent it to London to have it printed and it was published by T. Werner

Laurie at sevenpence per copy. Published is not really the right word, since the War Office took the whole print and nobody else has a copy. I have one, of course, and I know now that there is another copy in The War Museum. I had a letter from Marshal Templer telling me that he had seen a curious little paper-back about Russian for the English by A.L.S. but nobody at the Museum had any idea who A.L.S. was. He (Templer), of course, knew that they were my initials, but he could not imagine my having anything to do with such a book.

Incidentally, he is the only Knight of the Garter, so far as I know, who is a real gastronome. He joined the Wine and Food Society when it was founded, some thirty-odd years ago, as Captain Gerald Templer.

When Werner Laurie agreed to publish the little Russian grammar, I asked for two sets of galley proofs; one I corrected and sent back to the printer, and the other I sent, uncorrected, to no less a person than the Ministre de la Guerre, the Head of the French War Office, in Paris, asking for his permission to publish the little book. My letter did get to its destination in time, and in due course, it came back to me with the rubber stamp of all the official military departments through which it had had to go. The decision of the Deuxième Bureau (Intelligence) of the War Office was without appeal: the permit I had asked for could not be granted. It made no difference at all because the little book had been published and taken up by the War Office in England some four months earlier, but I have kept the letter with my postman's green card, as I was sure that nobody would believe the reason why Intelligence had come to their decision unless he read it for himself: first too many misprints; second, bad quality of the paper (galley proofs!). But we won the war all the same!

I had to wait until September 1916 to get my first home leave—three days only, three whole days. (Not, of course, counting the journey there and back.) Madeleine, the youngest of my five children, was only two years old in 1914, and howled when I tried to kiss her on the first day of my leave. On the second day, however, she let me kiss her and ran away; on the third day she spoke to me, not for long, but to some purpose: 'When are you going home?' she asked, with some concern. It so happened that the evening before I came home, my old friend A. S. Gardiner had been knocked down by a bus or car and was critically ill in Charing Cross Hospital, and the first thing I did on the first day of my leave was to go and see him. He was conscious and not only knew me but asked me if I would do something for him. Of course, I would be only too happy of a chance to do whatever he asked. Then he enquired if I would publish his cricket book. I said that I would, but thought that he was wandering. He never spoke again, but smiled and died. His wife came, but she came too late. I told her about his last words and she said that he had written, years ago, a little story 'The Autocrat of the Cricket Field' about their little son when he first played, as well as other short stories; he had often talked about publishing it. I knew then that he had been conscious to the last, and it gave me no pleasure, but a great satisfaction to publish *The Autocrat of the Cricket Field and The Old Crocks* by A. S. Gardiner, with a very good postscript. It was not much, but it had given him his last smile.

In June 1917 I was taken away from the fighting zone and sent as interpreter to the H.Q. of the Canadian Forestry Corps, at La Joux, in the Jura Mountains, between Pontarlier, on the Swiss border, and Arbois, where Pasteur was born. There were many casualties every day, but they were fir trees from the State forests of France in the Jura and Vosges, which the Canadian saw mills cut up to use for trenches and all kinds of military immediate and likely needs. It was a restful and interesting change of scene in a part of France hitherto unknown to me, but, needless to say, I was highly delighted when the news came

that I must go to London at once, having been appointed a
member of the French Secretariat to the Allied Maritime
Transport Council, the organization responsible for the
allocation of tonnage between the U.S.A., Great Britain and
France for their needs of food, munitions, and raw materials.
That was not only an interesting job, but it meant living
at home once again after three-and-a-half years!

The Council met in either London or Paris. When in
London Mr. Churchill was in the Chair; when in Paris,
M. Loucheur. I remember a meeting in Paris, at the Petit
Palais de la Légion d'Honneur, near the Quai d'Orsay
Hotel, when Loucheur as Chairman welcomed his two
chief guests, Churchill and Davies (U.S.A.) in French, and
gave a short speech about what he hoped would be done at
the meeting for the good of all. He ended by asking the
two guests, sitting at his right and left, if they wanted his
welcoming 'few words' in English. 'Non,' said Davies.
'S'il vous plaît,' said Churchill. So Loucheur made a sign
to the official interpreter, who read his shorthand notes in
French, which he translated into English as he went on,
when, much to my surprise, and I believe to the surprise of
everybody else in the room, Churchill stopped him and
corrected him; and he was right. To read French shorthand
just as if you were reading an English text is, of course,
extremely difficult, and the word which made Churchill
stop the interpreter was near enough to what Loucheur had
said, but it was not the exact word. I knew then that
Churchill's accent in French might be rather funny, but
that his knowledge of French was truly remarkable. He
was, of course, a very remarkable man!

On 11 November 1918, when the armistice was signed,
I believed that I would now immediately be set free to
return to my business, but Monsieur Clémentel, who was
at the time Ministre du Commerce, asked me to draft for
him what I thought should be embodied in the economic
clauses of the Peace Treaty to protect from unfair German

competition the wines and brandies of France. This did not take me very long to draft, and it was so simple that I hardly thought it would be accepted, but it was and I was told that the Germans had raised no objection to it when they signed the Versailles Treaty. My one and only 'Article' of the Peace Treaty was to the effect that the German Government undertook to introduce the necessary legislation to make the French provisions protecting the *Appellations contrôlées* equally binding in Germany by German law. What could be fairer than to ask the Germans to give to the wine-growers and merchants of France the same guarantees and protection which the laws of France accorded to the wine-growers and merchants of Germany.

VIII. FULL STOP. NEW CHAPTER

ARTHUR SPENCER was one of my oldest friends and neighbours in the City; I believe that the first drink I had with him and Toby Folks was in 1902, in his office, 26 Mark Lane. His firm was Walter Symons Ltd., not in a big way of business, and his staff was a young man whom he called Charles, although it was not his name, who inherited Walter Symons Ltd. at Spencer's death. Arthur Spencer was an old bachelor, intelligent and kind-hearted, with just one bee in his bonnet. He did not want anybody to know his age, or for that matter the date of his birthday. Some time at the end of February or early in March, he asked some of his friends, of whom I was one, to dine with him for his birthday at the Holborn, when oysters were at their best. Then we were sure to have another invitation from him at the end of August to a lunch at the National Liberal Club, again to celebrate his birthday when grouse were at their best.

I never had two birthdays, like Arthur Spencer, but I made it a habit to celebrate my name day, St. Andrew's Day, 30 November, as well as my birthday on 28 February. On 30 November 1932, we had the usual happy luncheon at 24 Mark Lane, with Champagne freely flowing and the host, poor me, doing his best to be cheerful although he really was on the verge of bursting into tears. I had received at midday on that day a short and plain letter informing me that after 31 December next my Reims firm would have nothing whatsoever to do with me and that they had given their agency to another firm who would not have anything to do with me either.

That was the price I had to pay for being unprepared for the first ever sterling devaluation! I bought Champagne, a great deal of it, in francs and sold it all over the world in sterling, which meant that overnight the amount of sterling due to me had so fallen in value that it did not add up to the amount of francs I owed to my Reims people. All I asked was to be given time. But I could not have it. It so happened that some friends of mine in the Wine Trade knew that I had many goodwill contacts which they believed would be of value to them, if they had my job, and they offered Reims to pay right away the balance of what I owed if they were given right away my job. They got it. That put the full stop to a chapter of thirty-three years' loyal service.

What was to happen next? Would there be another chapter? Of course, there had to be another chapter, but I little thought at the time that it would also be a chapter of another thirty-three years from 1933, when the Wine and Food Society was born, until May 1966, when I attended the first Convention of the Society, in Chicago. I am still nominally the Society's President, but I no longer have anything to do with its conduct and affairs.

When I lost my firm and my job I asked myself, and my friends asked me, what was to do now. I quite definitely told myself and told them that I would never again have anything to do with the Wine Trade. I had been writing for so many years at odd times, when I had a chance, but now I could and I would give the whole of my time and mind to what had been my lifetime hobby, not to call it my vocation.

And I meant it!

In the afternoon of 30 December 1932 a gentleman called, a total stranger who told us that his name was Julian Leacock and that he was a friend of one of my old friends who evidently knew what had happened to me and had told Julian Leacock about it. Anyhow, Julian Leacock's story was a simple one.

Julian and his wife were due to sail from Southampton on 2 January for a week's stay in Madeira. Julian wanted to see his aged mother, who lived there, and his brother, one of the island's wine shippers, on business. One of Julian's young sons had become ill, seriously enough for his mother to give up going to Madeira and to stay at home to look after him. Julian Leacock had come to ask me to come with him to and back from Madeira and to be for a week the guest of his brother and sister-in-law in the island. Of course, I refused, but my dear wife was so insistent and pressing that I must accept so providential an offer of a much needed change and thorough rest, that I gave in and sailed for Funchal two days later.

Both John Leacock and his wife were charming hosts and I had a most restful but by no means an idle week in Madeira.

Between 1919 and 1931 I went half a dozen times to the Cape by Union-Castle ships which, in those days, never failed to call and stay a day at Funchal where I came to know most of the English Madeira wine people; they had agents in London who gave me letters of introduction. That is how I met in 1920 the Blandys, who were the parents of the present older generation of Blandys. He was a great tree-lover, and so was I, and he had a wonderful collection of rare trees at the top of the hill N.N.E. of Funchal. His firm were shipping agents to various lines and some of their captains had for years brought Mr. Blandy specimens from odd parts of the world for his collection.

When I was asked to dinner by his widow in January 1934, I could not help telling my hostess how wonderful the Madeira was which we were drinking, and how grateful I was to her. 'Of course,' she said, 'I am giving you the best I have, but it is not the best there is in the island. Uncle Michael has the best there is; he does not drink it; he does not give it away; and he will not sell it.' Then she added, 'And he is ninety-three'; it sounded to me, by the tone of her voice, that she meant 'he is only ninety-three and likely to live to 100, but will the wine last?'

Uncle Michael's father was born in 1792, when wine of outstanding quality was made; some of it was sold as a special favour to the ex-Emperor Napoleon when his ship-prison stopped for fresh water and supplies at Funchal on her way to St. Helena. Napoleon's doctor found that he suffered from stomach ulcers and would not let him drink any Madeira, so the wine was sent back to Madeira, to the British Consul, M. Veitch, who had paid for it originally; he sold it to Charles Blandy, who left it to his son John, who gave it to his daughter and his son-in-law, Dr. Michael Grabham, who was born in 1840, when the wine was bottled. This is how Dr. Michael Grabham, in 1933, was ninety-three years old and the uncle of all the Blandys young and old. I had heard of Dr. Michael Grabham from my friend Sir Stephen Gaselee, the Librarian of the House of Lords, a Member of the Saintsbury Club and of the Funchal Club, loved by all in Madeira where he spent his yearly holiday.

The next evening, Sir Stephen and Lady Gaselee dined at St. John's, the Leacocks' home, where I was staying. She did not drink at all but he did, and he was particularly fond of old and very old wines. I told them the 1792 story which to my surprise Gaselee had not heard before. He asked me to lunch with him the next day and arranged that we would sit at Dr. Grabham's table. The old Doctor was a very remarkable man, much younger at ninety-three than I am now at ninety-two! Not only could he see quite well, whereas I am very nearly blind, but he still played the great organ whereas I would not know how to get any noise out of a tin whistle. I was absolutely charmed with him.

I never knew how Gaselee did it, what he told Uncle Michael about George Saintsbury and the *Notes on a Cellar Book*, and the Saintsbury Club, lately founded, but when Gaselee returned to London from Madeira that year dear old Dr. Michael Grabham had given him a dozen bottles of his so precious 1792. I believe that they were the last he had!

My dear wife did not know whether I was serious or joking when I told her on my return home that I was the Chairman of the Madeira Wine Association and that my job was to bring Madeira back into fashion!

Fickus, Courtenay were the first to offer me the use of the board room of their Savile Street Office as my office, but soon after William Burgess gave me a room as an office all to myself in Denman House, at the east corner of the Piccadilly Hotel. Quite a number of hotels, restaurants, stores, and others put some of my Madeiras on their wine lists, but there they remained; there was practically no demand, nor any funds for a publicity campaign. I quickly decided not to waste any more time on Madeira, and to put my trust, as I had originally intended, in printer's ink.

Michael Sadleir was the first friend to come forward with a helping hand. He proposed the publication by Constable of a series of inexpensive books dealing with the more popular wines under the title of 'Constable's Wine Library'. Some of the books were to be written by me and the others under my editorship. The first of the books dealt with Madeira; I only wrote the first part of it, all about the island and its wines. The rest of the book was written by Elizabeth Craig; it dealt with Madeira cake and Sauce Madère, as well as the best use to be made with Madeira in the kitchen. Although we did not mention any wine by the uncomplimentary name of cooking Madeira.

I wrote the next two books; one dealing with Champagne and the other with Port, two wines which could not be more different, yet both have in common that they are mostly known by the name of their shippers and not by the names of their vineyards.

I asked my oldest friend in the world of letters, H. Warner Allen, to write the book on Sherry, my devoted disciple

Maurice Healy the book on the wines of Bordeaux, Stephen Gwyn the Burgundy book, and Rudd, of Berry Bros., the book on Hocks and Moselle.

Nobody knew better than I did, because nobody had written more wine books than I had, that all books on wine soon get out of date. Which is why I had had for so long the hope or ambition to publish a monthly or quarterly periodical with articles keeping in step with the behaviour of the wines of different vintages after bottling.

I asked J. L. Garvin, the editor of the *Observer*, if he could give me half an hour or so as I wanted his advice, and he asked me to come to lunch with him and his daughter, on Sunday, at Beaconsfield. I did and explained to him what I had in mind. He was quite sure that a periodical dealing with wine was out of the question; the number of people, in England, outside the wine trade, who had their own cellars, was so small that the lay demand for a wine magazine would be insignificant. Wine was of interest to so few whilst millions wanted not only more food but to know more about food. Why not, he suggested, get all gourmets and gourmands into a Good Food Club, give them fine meals and make their annual subscription cover the cost of a monthly circular about the food of each month: all members might not want it or bother to read it but that would not matter; all would have to pay for the monthly copy.

Garvin's sound advice reminded me that I received four times a year *The Book Collector*, the quarterly magazine of the First Edition Club, of which I was a member. Indeed, I knew very well A. J. A. Symons, its founder, president, and secretary, whose *Quest for Corvo* made him famous. I asked him to lunch and he agreed with Garvin that food was more important than wine but he thought that my knowledge of wine might be of value if presented as food's partner. We talked it over on a number of occasions and finally decided to start a Society to be called the

Wine and Food Society 'to bring together and to serve all who took an intelligent interest in the problems and pleasures of the table'.

The first function to which our members were asked to come and to bring guests was a tasting of Madeira wines, a great many different wines, some very cheap for Sauce Madère, some good enough and reasonable in price, others from fine to great in both quality and cost, and finally a few quite priceless wines of the late eighteenth century, not for sale. Members and their guests could have as much of each wine as they wished and all they had to pay was three shillings and sixpence; that was for the hire of glasses and breakages; all the wines were given by the Madeira Wine Association. The second function was an Alsatian lunch at the Café Royal when the main dish was an excellent *Perdrix aux Chou*, all the wines given by Dopff of Riquewihr, no corkage to pay, and the inclusive cost ten shillings and sixpence. Then we had our first dinner; it was held at the Savoy, three good wines, fine fare and the inclusive cost one guinea. These first three Meetings, as we called all our functions, were entirely my own work, not too bad work, you may think, but I can tell you without any false modesty that what my friend and partner did was ever so much better. He had good friends in Fleet Street, youngish men of about his own age, like Tom Driberg, who had not been stung yet by the bug of politics and was the William Hickey of the *Daily Express*. A. J. A. Symons, not the Society, invited his friends, sat with them at table, talked to them intelligently and amusingly, and the next morning the Society had the most wonderful free publicity, not in *The Times*, but in other newspapers.

The number of new members who joined the Society averaged fifty per week, and when we reached one thousand in 1934, I knew that at long last I would soon publish the magazine I had been hoping for many years to edit.

Although A. J. A. Symons and I were so different from one another, we both believed that the best Committee is the Committee of two with one on holiday or in hospital. We felt quite able to look after the affairs of the Society by ourselves, but it was suggested to us that it would look somehow better if we had a list of names to show if and when we were asked who were the people who owned or ran the Wine and Food Society. So we asked some of our friends to become Members of our Advisory Council: it sounded more important than Committee. We never asked for their advice.

We had on our Advisory Council a Lord, Lord Moynihan, the one and only A.J.S.'s nominee. There was a Lord on the Council of the First Edition Club and A.J. thought that our Society should have one; maybe he was right but I never knew how or why Lord Moynihan agreed to give us his name. We also had a Lady, the Dowager Lady Swaythling, a dear friend of my wife and myself, at whose hospitable board we had so often discussed how to make a start and choose the right name for our proposed Society. All the other members of the Council were chosen by me as contributors to the Society's quarterly magazine. All of them had already written books or articles, so that I knew I could call upon them if or when in need. Henry Warner Allen came first alphabetically and in seniority of friendship; Professor Henry Armstrong, the youngest octogenarian that ever was; Marcel Boulestin, the first TV chef; Sir Francis Colchester-Wemyss; Maurice Healy; Elizabeth Craig; Ambrose Heath; Vyvyan Holland; G. B. Stern, and Sir Jack Squire.

As it happened, my friend A. J. A. Symons, twenty-two years younger than me, was taken ill in 1939 and died in 1941 leaving the Wine and Food Society to be carried on by me single handed. The Society still carries on, of course, and the quarterly magazine which I edited for nearly thirty years but sold to Condé Nast when I realized that old age had beaten me, is now a highly popular glossy magazine published six times a year with a world-wide circulation; all this is most gratifying. But as far as I am concerned the second thirty-three year chapter of my long life has come to an end.

E

IX. THE 'WINE AND FOOD' QUARTERLY

CHRISTMAS 1933 was for my family above all a day of thanksgiving. We had, indeed, good cause to be grateful when we remembered—and could we ever forget it!—how black and blank the previous Christmas had been. Now, one short year after, there was plenty of work waiting for me to do, and it was the sort of work which I knew I would enjoy doing, much more than having wine or anything else to boost and to sell against all comers, fair or unfair competitors.

Our new Society was very nearly five hundred strong already, and barely ten weeks old! It meant that my long-cherished ambition of having an editor's blue pencil of my own was within reach, and I was greatly elated at the thought that the publication of the magazine upon which I had set my heart would soon be an accomplished fact. I never had any doubt or fear of failure once a start had been made but I was far less certain about ways and means of making a start. How were we to pay the contributors who would write for us and the printers who would print the magazine? I had no capital left, but I was not without liquid assets altogether; I still had a very fair quantity of wine and, after a good deal of hesitation, I came to the decision to offer the contributors whom I had in mind to approach—there was, of course, not a single teetotaller among them—a tax-free 'reward' of wine, in lieu of payment in cash. And it worked. Authors like Hilaire Belloc and G. B. Stern would have looked upon a cheque for five guineas as an insult, but they could and did accept a dozen bottles of Château-bottled Claret, not only with good grace but with thanks, in no way concerned by the fact that at the time a dozen bottles of Château-bottled Claret cost less than five guineas. This settled one problem only; the other, how the printer was to be paid, was still unsolved. What made matters more difficult was A.J.'s insistence that the members should be *given* the Society's magazine, as an inducement for them to join. He argued that he had sufficient experience, when publishing the *Book Collector's Quarterly*, which was given to all members of the First Edition Club, to know that there were comparatively few people who had both the inclination and the time to read a specialized periodical, however interesting it might be: hence his conviction that if members of the Wine and Food Society, who had paid one guinea to belong to it, were asked to pay a further fifty per cent, or half a guinea more, for a magazine which, he said, most of them did not want and never expected to have the time to read, they might quite naturally imagine that their membership of the Society was going to lead them into all manner of expenses, and they would not be so keen to belong to it.

I bowed to his greater publishing experience, and, after a great deal more hesitation, I decided that I had no choice but to appeal, however much I might dislike it, to my friends of my Wine Trade days. I shall never forget their generous response. Willie Todd, for instance, was not satisfied to take a page advertisement for 'the duration' of the proposed quarterly magazine, but he insisted on presenting me with a cheque for one hundred pounds towards initial expenses. Ian Campbell, Sir Ernest Rutherford, Victor Seyd, Toby Folks, Price Hallowes, Ronnie Fox and other old competitors of mine among the Champagne shippers took 'space' for the first four numbers of the magazine; F. Gummer for Dolamore, Jumbo Jolliffe for Booth, Hodsoll for Grierson & Oldham, Martell and Hennessy and a number of Port and Sherry agents, Brandy and Liqueurs shippers, as well as the Savoy, the Carlton, Grosvenor House, Holborn and Frascati, and other London hotels and restaurants advertised, besides the Hind's Head Hotel at Bray, whose page advertisement has never failed once to be a feature of *Wine and Food* from the first number to the latest out.

The first year of publication of any periodical is bound to be an experimental stage, and it is often a critical one. Although I realize that I am running the risk of being chided for singing my own praises, I cannot help challenging anyone to deny that *Wine and Food* had won recognition and had established itself after its first year, with the four numbers published in 1934. This initial success was greatly due to the wholehearted support which was given to me by a score of men, and one lady, people of good sense and good taste, whose abhorrence of mediocrity was as sincere as it was articulate: most of them were members of the Saintsbury Club, such as Hilaire Belloc, Professor Henry D. Armstrong, Ian M. Campbell, Stephen Gwynn, Ernest Oldmeadow, Horace Annesley Vachell, and Dr. George W. Williamson, who were all older than I was; and among other members who were junior to me, Martin Armstrong, the gentle poet, Edward Bunyard, the fruit specialist, A. Duff Cooper, the late Lord Norwich, Stephen Gaselee, Maurice Healy, Vyvyan Holland and Ralph Straus, the *Prattler*, the *Idler* and the *Scribbler* of the *Odd Volumes*. It was a truly magnificent team for any editor, besides a number of other personal friends who were also gifted writers, such as Marcel Boulestin, E. G. Boulenger, Louis Golding, Ambrose Heath and our one and only lady contributor, G. B. Stern.

The success of *Wine and Food* was so gratifying that we decided to probe further this source of revenue, and also of prestige, and we published two little paper-cover books. The first, in 1934, was entitled *The Wine Connoisseur's Catechism*; it was a brought-up-to-date reprint of *The Wine Connoisseur*, a booklet that I had written some years before for the Education Committee of the Wine Trade Club; the other, a fatter book, published in 1935 at two shillings, whereas the *Catechism* cost one shilling only, was entitled *Wines and Liqueurs from A to Z*: it was a simple glossary which has proved very popular from the time when it was first published up to now.

To get good writers to write good articles, and to get good printers to print them well is a promising start, but a starting line is a very long way from the winning post. The great difficulty is to get a book 'out', to have it published by specialists who have the means and profit motive to place it before the right reading public. Naturally, neither A.J. nor I had the first notion how to do it, nor had we any of the indispensable facilities for the distribution of our magazine and books. Hence our obligation to find a publisher who could handle our publications for us. We could, of course, and we did post to our members their 'gift' copy of the quarterly every quarter, but we were most anxious that the magazine should be available to the public, in the best booksellers' shops and on the bookstalls. The problem of finding a publisher always has been a very important as well as a most difficult one for us, and its importance as well as its difficulties were more obvious, not to say ominous, to A.J. than they were to me. He was very anxious that we should get the co-operation of a well-established publisher who would do for *Wine and Food* what Cassell had done for the *Book Collector's Quarterly*: it would have meant that I would have had an entirely free hand as regards the editorial contents and policy of the magazine, but the publisher, when we had found one, would have been responsible for all financial liabilities, as well as attending, of course, to the sale and circulation of the magazine. A.J. talked it over with his friend Michael Fletcher, and convinced him that the publication of the magazine which we had in mind could not fail to be a source of added prestige as well as financial gain for Michael Fletcher's firm. Michael Fletcher was the editor of a

well-known and prosperous medical periodical owned by a
popular Member of Parliament, Brendan Bracken, who
had come to lunch at 24 Mark Lane the year before. On
24 November 1933, A.J. and I entertained Brendan Bracken
and Michael Fletcher to lunch at the Café Royal. Both A.J.
and I had great hopes that we were to come to terms and
clear the tallest, if not the last, of the hurdles in our way
to the winning post. The day was a Friday and I had taken
great pains to make it a memorable meatless meal, regard-
less of cost—which meant a lot to us both at a time when
we were very poor. We began with a dozen each of the
best Whitstable Oysters, and we partnered them with a
Riesling 1929 of Dopff's shipping. Then came a delicious
Omelette fourrée au Crabe, a moist omelette with a plentiful
filling of the white meat only of freshly boiled crabs, topped
with a light Sauce Mornay browned under the *Salamandre*
just before serving. The main dish was a *Buisson d'Ecrevisses à la nage*, a great dish of scarlet, fat little crayfish, which
were said to have been caught in the Colne River: whether
home-caught or imported from Poland was not so important; they were excellent. With both the omelette and
the crayfish we drank a 1919 Musigny Blanc of the
Marquis de Vogüé's bottling. We ended with a Brie
cartwheel: the cheese was in prime condition, just starting
to be runny and not too assertive of taste—it made a
perfect match for the Château Latour 1923 which we
drank with it. Of course, the coffee was *double*, if not
triple and as *pousse-café* we had one of the half-bottles of
Denis Mounié 1830, bottled at the Café Royal at the heyday
of its gastronomic fame. I have had many good meatless
meals in my life but I do not remember any that was
better, and very few indeed that were as good as this
Café Royal lunch. Unfortunately, nothing came of it,
except vague promises and wasted time.

When we had no doubt left that Brendan Bracken was,
as far as we were concerned, a broken reed, Curwen were

about to print our first number of *Wine and Food*, and A.J. arranged in somewhat of a hurry with Simpkin Marshall & Co. that they were to 'publish' our magazine for us, which meant attending to its distribution but leaving us to pay the printers and being entirely responsible financially. It was, however, the best we could do and there is no doubt that the choice of Simpkin Marshall was a very good one: we sold through them a fair number of copies of *Wine and Food* to a few of the more enterprising booksellers, but practically none on the bookstalls. This was not the fault of the publishers, however; it was due to the fact that bookstall attendants soon realized that the demand of the travelling public for a new magazine with an appeal which was limited by its very title was too small to justify giving it space that could be occupied much more profitably by more popular publications.

As regards the advertising revenue from *Wine and Food*, A.J. was not so lucky; he gave the contract to a Fleet Street firm which came to grief within the year and although our loss was not very great in itself it was one which we could ill afford. Happily, thanks to George Messenger who had introduced me to Sir Harold Harmsworth, *The Field* agreed to attend to both the publishing and the publicity of *Wine and Food* from March 1935, and they did both so well that we were not only spared all further anxiety, but we had the great satisfaction of seeing the circulation of *Wine and Food* and its advertising revenue rise steadily from year to year, until the end of 1939.

X. THE UNITED STATES

THE weather in the Bay of Biscay is unpredictable. It can
be all sunshine and the gentlest breeze, but it can also
be a mass of battling great wild waves whipped by howling
winds. Equally unpredictable is the weather of Bordeaux
and its rolling sea of vineyards facing the Bay. The weather
on land, however, is of incomparably greater importance,
since it is responsible for bad, good, fair, fine, and great
wines. In 1928 and 1929, for instance, there was a great
deal of wine, most of it of fine quality, to gladden the hearts
and pay off the debts of the Bordeaux vignerons. Then came
the catastrophe of three bad vintages: 1930, 1931, and 1932.
It was a bad enough financial blow for the merchants; they
had stocks of 1928 and 1929 wines, happily, but their over-
heads were the same in good and bad vintages. For the
vignerons who lived from year to year from the sale of the
grapes of the year, it was stark ruin or putting their neck
in the bankers' noose! The customary Happy New Year
and good wishes sounded like a mockery, in the Bordeaux
vinelands, in January 1933. Yet it turned out to be a happy
—or at any rate a happier—new year. A ray of real sunshine
came across the Atlantic! The news that the Volstead Act
was to be repealed was taken, in Bordeaux, to mean the end
of Prohibition, and the end of Prohibition was taken for
granted by many, with greater haste than common sense,
to mean a flood of orders for the wines of Bordeaux. The
unsold poor wines of 1930, 1931, and 1932 were no longer
unsaleable and quotations for the 1928 and 1929 vintages
rose sharply. In the winter of 1933–34, and in the spring
of 1934, the proprietors of many famous vineyards and the
heads or senior members of important wine firms, from

Champagne and Burgundy, and many more from Bordeaux than anywhere else, sailed for the U.S.A. full of hope and joy. They all came back full of gloom; they had lost their time, their money, and their illusions; the Americans showed little interest, and certainly no enthusiasm for wine. This is not imagination on my part but what was told to me by Jean Couprie, the Secrétaire Général de la Commission d'Exportation des Vins de France, in July 1934, at Bidart, near Biarritz, where my wife and I, our daughter Jeanne and her little son were enjoying a holiday at La Malika, Alice Delysia's charming house, which she had lent to us. Jean Couprie was no stranger; I had been Vice-President of the Commission d'Exportation for some years, in the twenties, and we were old friends. He had come all the way from Paris to ask me, on behalf of the Commission's Comité, to go to the United States and boost the wines of France. I said 'No' right away and pointed out to him that his request was preposterous; had he not just told me that all the members of the Commission who had been to the States for that very purpose had failed? What chance of better luck had I? He would not take 'No' for an answer; he begged of me to think it over and write to him; this is what I promised him to do, and did.

I had never been to the States; it certainly was no place for me during Prohibition! It seemed to me obvious, however, that the rich or well-to-do Americans who were the more likely to buy imported, hence expensive wines, were the young or youngish ones, in their twenties, thirties and early forties, whether they entertained or were entertained at home or in restaurants and luxury hotels. It also seemed obvious to me that the older ones had been too young, before Prohibition, to take any interest in wine, and that the others, who came to manhood or womanhood during the years of Prohibition, might well have acquired a holy horror of alcohol and alcoholics, and that between those two extremes, there was a much greater number of more sensible people who knew that a few cocktails before the meal helped conversation and conviviality. I could well imagine that wine with meals, even in the homes of the wealthy, might well have become old fashioned, a boring text for elderly retired financiers and others who loved to talk of the great cellars when those were the days. All that, or most of it, was guess work on my part, and after talking it over with my wife—I might even say chiefly on her advice—I decided to go and see for myself whether it was possible or not to make an élite of American people of taste appreciate how much better a meal is when good food is partnered with the right wine instead of iced water.

Then I wrote to Jean Couprie, as promised. I told him that we had started, in London, a Society called Wine and Food, which meant wine with food; its object was to make more people take a more intelligent interest in what they ate and drank, and to appreciate that all food, served with good wine and enjoyed in the company of good friends, belonged to a sensible, cultured and gracious way of living. I told him that, in spite of very unfavourable conditions, we had already over 1,000 members. I told him that I was prepared to go to the States, not to boost French wines, but to find, if possible, the right type of American willing and able to run Wine and Food Societies in all important cities of the United States, planning and giving dinners, luncheons and tastings for the pleasure and education of their members. I would, of course, do my best to show them how to do it, as well as get as much publicity as I could for Wine—all wines, not French wine only.

I had Couprie's reply soon after; the Comité agreed and hoped that my wife and I would sail for New York as soon as possible. I booked our passage by the French Line's not very new but still very good ship *Paris*, not because she bore the name of my native village, but because she was due to sail from Le Havre on 13 November, and I knew that I could not be ready to go any earlier. I had to prepare the programme of the London Society's functions during my absence; I had to see the September quarterly through the press, and put together what would be the December number, and make sure that I would be leaving all my affairs in good order before leaving.

On 13 November, as *Paris* sailed from Le Havre, my wife and I were the guests of the Wine and Food Society at a Farewell and Goodwill Banquet at the Savoy. Besides members of the Society and their guests, and members of the Press, most of the wine-producing countries of Western Europe, France, Italy, Spain, and Portugal were represented by their ambassadors; Germany, Switzerland and Luxembourg by their *chargés d'affaire*. We were 495 in all, and my old friend Colonel Ian M. Campbell of Airds was in the Chair. I never had before or since as fine fare at a great banquet as we had that evening. It was Francis Latry's best ever!

On 15 November we went by train to Plymouth where *Paris* was awaiting our arrival, and a few days later we were admiring the New York sky-scrapers as we sailed slowly up the Hudson, on a cold, crisp, clear early afternoon.

We had very comfortable quarters on the thirty-fourth floor of the Hotel Pierre, and a very busy but most disappointing time in New York. I had, of course, collected a number of introductions and I do not think that my wife and I ever had a *tête-à-tête* meal! We entertained and we were entertained a great deal but somehow we failed to meet the right people, that is people with a sufficient knowledge and love of wine to give the time and take the trouble to choose the right wines for a dinner or a tasting as well as the right place where such a dinner or tasting had best be held; then let all members know the time, place and cost of any such functions, and all this without any financial reward whatsoever. It is certainly a lot to ask anybody, but such people do exist, enough of them to run over one hundred Branches of our Society in different parts of the world.

We left New York early in December, not despondent but rather depressed, for Boston, where we were to be the guests of Sohier and Mrs. Welch. Much to our surprise and delight we found that our Boston friends had more to teach us than we could teach them. Sohier Welch, Gus Loring, Charlie Codman and a few more had already started a dining club which they called Le Club des Arts Gastrono-miques. All were true wine lovers, and although Charlie Codman was in charge of the wine department of Boston's finest department store, it only meant that he knew more about wine than his friends; he was as unprejudiced as any of them. The dinners of the Club des Arts Gastronomiques were limited to seven men; no ladies.

To find, in Boston, those few men who were genuine wine lovers was not only a great surprise for me but a tonic, but the greatest gift of Providence was Theodora. She was the dynamic and highly intelligent wife of Charlie Codman, and she realized at once that a Boston Wine and Food Society would do far more for the recognition and apprecia-tion of wine than the dinners of the Club des Arts Gas-tronomiques for a few men only. It was really Theodora Codman, not me, who started the Boston Chapter of the Society. Gus Loring was the President, benevolent, amiable, Pickwickian somewhat and lovable, but Theodora was the Hon. Secretary, quick, efficient, the 'no nonsense' type of woman who gets things done, and well done, but does not expect and rarely gets a thank you.

Theodora and the Boston Chapter have had for many years, and still have, a special place in my heart. Boston was the first of the few American Chapters of the Society where ladies and gentlemen enjoy each other's company at the Society's dinners and tastings, in the conventional civilized manner.

Our stay in Boston was very short, but it was a success beyond hope. We returned to New York in a much happier mood than we had left it. We soon left it again for California, where we hoped to find warmth and sunshine. On the way we stopped in Chicago. I had every hope of meeting another Theodora Codman, Suzette Dewey, who not only took an intelligent interest in wine but had actually written and published, in 1934, a charming little book on wines, a copy of which she had sent to me. The Deweys were truly delightful people who came to France every year for a holiday; they had a house in Normandy. A Chicago Chapter of the Society with Suzette Dewey as Hon. Secretary would have brought together many if not most of the much travelled and highly cultured men and women of Illinois around Chicago. But it was not to be. They entertained us generously on our arrival but told us that they were leaving Chicago very shortly for Washington as Mr. Dewey was now a senator. With greater haste than sense, I asked Arnold Shircliffe to take charge of a Chicago Chapter of the Society. He was a Birmingham-born American citizen with a rather important job in the catering trade. As a subscriber to one or the other of the Wine Trade journals published in London, he had read about the Wine and Food Society and had sent his three dollars to become a member; he was the first member the Society had in the United States, and he had written to me, when we were in New York, asking me to let him know when I would be in Chicago; which, naturally, I did. He could not have been kinder to us nor worked harder for the Society, but he was not really the right type for the job. We left Chicago a week before Christmas for San Francisco where we had better luck. It so happened that the French Trade Counsellor in California was Melchior de Polignac's former private secretary Ernest Guy, who had since married a French cousin of mine. It made all the difference! He introduced me to the right people so there was soon a San Francisco Chapter of the Society with Harold Price as its enthusiastic and able Hon. Secretary. There we met a number of the vineyard-owners, none more hospitable than Georges de Latour and his wife, whose vineyard and winery at Beaulieu had managed somehow to carry on during the Prohibition years.

From San Francisco, where my wife caught a chill, we moved to Los Angeles, where she would have died of double pneumonia had it not been for the skill and devotion of Dr. Pepper, the hotel doctor. I was fortunate to meet a number of willing helpers and to start the Southern California Chapter of the Society with Phil Townsend Hanna as Hon. Secretary and William Converse as Chairman. There also we met Jack and Helen Garland whose friendship and affection we enjoyed for many years; they never failed to visit us when they came to London, every year, until my wife's death, in 1963, and to come and see me, at Little Hedgecourt, until they died within a few days of each other, in 1969.

After a short period of rest and convalescence in the sunshine of Palm Springs, we moved to New Orleans, where the tradition of gastronomy and *la joie de vivre* is probably older than anywhere else in the United States. The idea of a New Orleans Wine and Food Society was hailed with enthusiasm and the first Dinner held Chez Antoine in Mi-Carême style! Roy Alciatore was in charge.

Back in New York for a short spell before returning to England, I was pleased to see that some of the seeds scattered during our first stay there had taken root and borne fruit. There was a New York Chapter of the Wine and Food Society, with Mr. Taft, a brother of the former President of the U.S.A., as President, Robert J. Misch as Hon. Secretary, and Crosby Gaige as Chairman of the Committee; none of them knew anything about wine, but they could trust implicitly the counsels and guidance of Freddie Wildman, a really knowledgeable wine lover and wine-merchant.

Having been obliged to cut down my first American tour, owing to my wife's illness, I returned to the States, in 1935, alone and by air. I visited a dozen or more cities, gave dinners and talks, had many promises. But there are only two Chapters of the Society today which date back to 1935: Kansas City and Baltimore. I am still hearing from time to time from my old friend Harry Fawcett, for many years the Secretary of the Kansas City Club, where I was his guest, in 1935, when we started the Kansas City Chapter of the Society. I am very sorry that Philip Stieff is no more; he and his wife were such good friends of mine. Their home was my home whenever I went to Baltimore. He did so much for the Baltimore Chapter of the Society that it nearly died when he died, but happily it survived and is now, I am told, flourishing again.

I paid four more visits to the States before the war, the last time in May 1939, by *Normandie*, of the French Line, the finest passenger ship ever built since Noah's Ark. Crossing the Atlantic on or in *Normandie*, which I had the good fortune to do three times in all, was for me a real joy ranking now among the happiest memories of my life.

Remembering the excellence of the fare on board *Normandie* brought back to my mind a rather amusing incident of my first flight to and back from New York, in 1935. I was at the New York airport in the queue waiting to board the plane that was to land us the next morning—it was then about 7 p.m. New York time—after two stops, as was done in those days, the first at Gander and the other at Shannon, when the chief catering officer of the A.A. (American Air Lines), to whom I had been introduced when I had been to the A.A. New York City Office to check my ticket, came to me and asked me if I had checked my luggage. I told him that I had. 'Come along with me,' he said, and I did. He took me up into my plane and showed me with pride the electric grill which was to be used almost as soon as we would be airborne for the first time in the A.A. Line's history to cook a pile of red, raw cutlets for our dinner. Then he said goodbye and I settled down in my seat as my fellow passengers were coming up the gangway. We took off quite nicely and it was not long before the air hostess came along with a tray and offered us Sherry or a Cocktail. That was the usual opening gambit. The next thing that I expected was to have the small tray-table fitted on the back of the armchair immediately in front of me let down ready for my dinner. But that did not happen, and the hostess reappeared with the same tray and another lot of Sherries or Cocktails. I knew that something must have gone wrong. I got up and went to see the chef. He was almost in tears. The grill had fused and he could not get it to work. So presently the loud speaker announced that something had gone astray with our dinner, but Gander had been warned and there would be a hot dinner for us on arrival. It so happened that when we reached Gander another plane also touched down, but coming from London, so that two buses, with passengers from both planes, came to the one and only Cafeteria at the same time. There was a man at the entrance of the main hall with slips of paper or tickets in two different colours, and he asked all comers whether bound for New York or London. 'What difference does it make?' I asked. 'If you have come from New York, you will have a late dinner, pork chops and baked beans; but if you are going to New York you will have an early breakfast, eggs and bacon.' I said that I was going to New York; a lie, I know; not a white lie but a pardonable lie, as I thought at the time—and still think.

About a year later, the French consul in London rang me up and wanted to know what I had been up to; he had heard from the American consul in London that the whole of the American police had been hunting for me in vain! It was the fault of the A.A. catering man who had taken me from the waiting queue before I had passed before the immigration official who would have duly noted my exit; failing this, I was presumed to be still in the States, illegally and in hiding!

During the war, the American members of the Society kept up their subscription to the Society's quarterly *Wine and Food*, which is all they had ever been asked to pay, and I was most grateful to them; it was thanks to them that we were able to get paper from the Paper Control Board, and that I was able to boast that during my thirty years as editor of our quarterly, war or no war, it never failed once to be published on the due date.

In 1946, Crosby Gaige wrote to me, asking me to come as soon as possible, and stay as long as possible. He wanted to talk over with me a wonderful plan which he had 'perfected' during the war years to make the great American public drink wine, be more sober, more cultured and very much happier. Money was no problem, he added, which made the whole story more rather than less difficult to accept as a serious proposition. But Crosby really meant it all. I had a reply paid cable from him asking for the date of my coming so that my air ticket might be sent to me. So I went.

The first thing which Crosby showed me, when I arrived in New York, was not his famous plan but my book of tickets for a flying tour of a number of the more important cities of the Union. Frank Schoonmaker had the same and we were to go together and get people interested in wine in each city. We were given introductions, met some nice people, had some good meals, but did no good at all. Crosby's plan was just verbose imagination, and yet he had managed to get Frank's and my expenses paid by a wealthy firm of distillers with a unique chain of wine and spirit distributing shops all over the land. The only part of Crosby's plan which I did admire was its full morocco binding!

When I think of the time and money I spent in the United States, during some thirty years of my life, on and off; of all the labour of love and pep talks I gave in the cause of wine, I cannot help being tempted to call it a failure until I remember that once upon a time I was a gardener, as my friends know who knew Little Hedgecourt years ago, and a gardener must have faith and patience. The Wine and Food Society has now blossomed beautifully, and it has

F

become a national institution. I like to imagine that my early work was of some help, but I do realize, of course, that it is really due to a gardener of genius, Dr. George Rezek, and his team, true lovers of wine all.

My failure (since never having more than twenty Chapters of the Society in the States, twelve of them in California, can be called a failure) was due to the fact that I did not meet anybody of the Rezek type, an extremely rare type, unfortunately. I did meet true lovers of wine, one more knowledgeable about wine than either Dr. Rezek or myself; I mean Maynard Amerine, of course, whose books on wine are easily the best there are in the English language; but his work at the University of California left him no chance for the kind of missionary crusading in the Rezek style even had the gift been his.

Happily, during my visits to the United States, I made more friends than I started Chapters of the Wine and Food Society, in and out of the wine and catering trades, more especially among bookish men. I have been for many years and I am still an honorary member of the Boston Odd Volumes and of the Los Angeles Zamoranos—the original Zamorano was the Spaniard-printer who had the first printing press in California.

One of the penalties of living as long as I have is that one outlives most of one's old friends or loses contact. In New York, I have known longer than anybody else Bob Misch who has come to see me at Little Hedgecourt, with his wife Janet, and daughter Mary. There is now in New York, I am told, a very active and popular Chapter of our Society, conducted in the right and proper manner by the right people. This gives me the greatest possible satisfaction. Much as I loved dear Jeanne Owen, I entirely disagreed with her way of conducting single-handed and in a high-handed manner the New York Wine and Food Society.

In Boston, where I had once upon a time such good friends, I have none now, but in Baltimore I still have an

old and very dear friend, Harold Leonardt, happily a
regular visitor to London and a very generous host. Frank
and Romilla Gould are, since the death of Jack and Helen
Garland, in 1969, the last of my old friends in California.
But I must not forget that the young man whom I first
met in Boston many years ago, also once in Baltimore, when
he asked me to give a talk on wine at the City Hospital, not
to the sick or the alcoholics, but to the nurses, is now
Dr. Robert Knudsen of San Francisco. Postwar but old
friends who come to London fairly regularly are my dear
Helen and Harry Johnson. He is my one and only model
American correspondent.

The last time I visited the States was in May 1966 for
the first Convention of the Wine and Food Society. But that
is another story.

XI. MEMORABLE MEALS

MANY, indeed, are the meals which it has been my good fortune to enjoy, as host or as guest, in the course of my long and well-wined life; meals deserving to be gratefully remembered—Memorable Meals.

Many of those meals were published in book form, by Constable, in 1933 as *Tables of Content*, a title that was suggested by my dearly beloved disciple Maurice Healy. A great many more have been published in the Wine and Food Society's magazine *Wine and Food* from 1934 to 1963, including the austerity years of the war and the immediate post-war period. There are, however, quite a number of other meals which deserve to be called 'memorable' since I still remember them, although not because of their gastronomic excellence, like the others, but on account of some exceptional circumstance or unexpected feature which had little or nothing to do with wine and food.

For instance, I have not the faintest recollection of the fare given at the New Gaiety Restaurant, in London, about 1910, but I remember the occasion as if it had been last week, just because there was an unusual or unique feature which stamped itself in my mind and made the meal memorable; it happened to be the man in the chair that evening.

The night before the New Gaiety Restaurant was opened to the public was the scene of a very gay and brilliant 'guests'' dinner. The London agents of all the leading Champagne firms had been invited, as well they deserved to be, since they had all donated a dozen of their best vintage wine to the management. I had been asked to lunch that morning by Oscar Philippe of the Cavour, and

on my way to Leicester Square I looked in at the New
Gaiety to make sure that all was well and that there would
be no hitch in the evening. It was a lucky precaution. There
was in the middle of the room a great horse-shoe table for
our party with a fine armchair for the chairman at the
top of the table. I told Nobile, who was the New Gaiety
manager, that he must remove that armchair as we wanted
to sit all together with no chairman. Nobile told me quite
sensibly that we were too many for a round table, and that
he would put an ordinary chair in place of the armchair,
if I wished, but he could not help a horse-shoe table having
a centre seat at the bend. I was obliged to agree that it was
so and told him to leave the armchair where it was, but I
was rather worried about it, knowing as I did how difficult
it was going to be to choose one of us to sit in that armchair
without hurting the susceptibilities of the others. And so
to the Cavour I went to lunch with my problem unsolved.
It happened that Philippe had another guest besides myself:
his butcher. His butcher was a Mr. Dale, who was also a
farmer and who lived at Bournemouth: he was quite deaf
but otherwise a nice old fellow, and the thought occurred
to me that he would be just the man to put in the Chair
that evening to preside over the Champagne boys' party.
We had been talking about the opening of this latest of the
London restaurants, which promised to be the smartest of
them all, and I was delighted when Mr. Dale agreed to stay
in London overnight and be my guest that evening. He was
a little surprised to be given such a place of honour, but his
surprise was nothing compared to that of everybody else.
Guests and staff fired all sorts of questions at the Chairman,
but he heard none of them and his only reply was a benign
smile; never a word.

Another memorable meal which had nothing to do with
food or wine was made unforgettable by its date and place:
the date was 18 June 1915, the centenary of Waterloo,
and the place was Flanders. I was at the time attached to the

50th (Northumbrian) Division as interpreter and there was little I could interpret, as I knew not a word of Flemish, but I did my best to make up for it by raising the standard of the gastronomic reputation of our mess. It was very low, and no wonder, since the man who had been fitted out to cook for us was by vocation, choice, or accident a Leeds dustman; his one asset—which did not help him in our mess—was that his wife was a very good cook. He was willing to learn, however, and no fool, so there was some progress made. By a lucky chance the 50th Division moved out of Flanders into France on 19 June, so that on the 18th we were out of the front line, not at peace, nor exactly at war, but able to sit down to a really special meal in a barn with a roof on, and no windows, so that we could have as many lighted candles as we wished, and we did not care if it rained. It was not the fare that was memorable, but the occasion, and by the time we went to sleep that night we all felt confident that we would win the war very soon and be home for good by Christmas! This was the menu:

Consommé au Shrapnel

Saumon de Tin   A. & Q. Sauce

Epaule d'Agneau Wellington (N.Z.)
Pommes Nouvelles
Petits Pois Poperinghois

Terrine de Foie Gras aux Truffes
Cœurs de Laitues

Macédoine de Fruits à la Quatre-Bras

Canapé Saillant d'Ypres

Fraises Napoléon

Vins: Gonzalez' Amontillado
        Berncasteler 1904
        Pommery & Greno
        Graham's Five Crowns Port and Waterloo Cup

Toasts: The King: Colonel C.M.C.
　　　　 The Allies: Lt.-Colonel E.P.
　　　　 The Duke: A.L.S.
　　　　 L'Empereur: Major A.E.H.
　　　　 The Ladies: Major T.D.

A meal which was made memorable by the visit of one guest and the rudeness of another was a lunch which I gave at the Ecu de France in the mid-thirties to Maurice Healy and a well-known novelist whom I had not met before. My two guests arrived together, and as I was telling Maurice that I had had two Clarets decanted for our lunch, one fairly young and the other fairly old, my other guest declared in no uncertain manner that he did not care for Claret, that he wanted Champagne and that it had to be Clicquot, his favourite brand. He got it and spoke no more until dear Maurice, who was doing his best to make conversation and to make an unpropitious occasion a little less strained, said 'Believe it or not, I have quite a gift for recognizing a man's nationality. That little waiter who waits upon us, I can tell you is a Frenchman.' 'Of course he is,' blurted my plain-speaking other guest, 'they are all French waiters here.' 'Wait a moment,' Maurice said gently, 'let me finish. He is not only a Frenchman, he is a Bourguignon; of that I am certain, but I am also fairly sure that he is from Dijon, the typical Dijonnais type.' At that moment, our waiter came to remove our plates and I asked him where he came from. 'Moi, Monsieur? Istanbul,' was his prompt reply. None of us showed any surprise, but as he walked away with our plates, dear Maurice shook his head and said to himself, but loudly enough for both of us to hear, in a most compassionate tone, too funny for words: 'Poor little bastard, he does not know.' Well, it did what Maurice had been trying to do—it made my rude guest smile and start talking in a more civilized manner. It is only fair to add, however, that he was a sick man and not his real self. He died a fortnight later.

Another meal, the fare of which was probably simple and good, but long since forgotten, was made memorable by the place, the great Pasteur's house in Versailles, and the hosts, Madame Vallery-Radot, Pasteur's only daughter, her husband and their son, Pasteur's only grandson. He had been our guest at Evelyn Mansions before, in 1922, when he had come for the celebrations on the occasion of Pasteur's centenary. The Versailles house was at the time a Pasteur Museum. The small, very simply furnished room which had been the great man's bedroom was still exactly as it had been the day he died, with his watch and rosary on top of a small night table by the bed. In the drawing room, in a great sloping sort of desk, under glass, were displayed the many gold medals and silk *cravates* of the many Orders and Honours from many countries for all to see and admire. But what my wife, our two elder daughters, Jeanne and Marcelle, and myself were privileged to be given were the last bottles of Château Lafite which the Rothschild of his day had given Louis Pasteur. I am sorry to say that the occasion was more memorable than the wines themselves. It is not usual, but it is possible for great men to make great mistakes, and as far as I know the great Pasteur never made but one great mistake: he did not drink the wines given to him by the Rothschilds before he died!

Louis Bower, Lord Mayor of London, was a wine-merchant, a customer of a friend of mine. When he paid an official visit to Verdun, I went with him as far as Reims, where we dined and stayed at the Château des Craigères as the guests of the Marquis de Polignac. Earlier in the day, however, the Maire of Reims had given a Vin d'Honneur as a welcome to the Lord Mayor of London, not at the Hôtel de Ville, a sad sight indeed, still a blackened shell— a victim of the war. Bower had with him two men from the Guildhall in their best liveries; Jim who was rather tall, thin and slow, and Tom who was shorter, redder in the face and quicker both in movement and of wit. They were to make sure that the Lord Mayor was rightly dressed and generally look after him. In the great hall where they had the Vin d'Honneur (I believe that it had been formerly the residence of the Archbishops of Reims) Jim and Tom stood at attention behind their master as the Maire of Reims made his welcoming speech in English. There were glasses for everybody, including Jim and Tom, of course, and a great popping of corks. When all glasses were filled, the Lord Mayor of London read his speech in French. When he stopped, there were cheers, more Champagne, and we should have left, had it not been for a stupid Mr. Know-all who called for a speech from the sheriffs: he had evidently heard that there were two sheriffs as well as the Lord Mayor of London, and he had taken for granted that they had come with him. In no time everybody in the room joined in calling for the sheriffs. Louis Bower looked worried and obviously did not understand at all what all the fuss was about, but I did, and so did Tom. He stepped forward and stretched out both arms. In his right hand was an empty glass which was immediately filled with Champagne. Silence was complete and Tom spoke for the sheriffs. His speech was short; six words only, which I still remember quite clearly: 'God bless France and damn prohibition.' Then 'down the hatch!' He fairly poured his full glass of Champagne down his throat. There was a thunder of cheers but I grabbed Tom's glass rather rudely out of his hand, and told him that we were getting late and must go. I do not know for sure, but I am quite ready to believe that Mr. Know-all told all his friends that Tom would be the next Lord Mayor of London!

I have had a greater number of memorable meals of superlative excellence at the Savoy, during the past seventy years, than anywhere else in London, chiefly during the years when my friend Francis Latry was the chef. Yet the meal which may be called truly memorable, since it is clear in my memory after very nearly fifty years, is the most uninteresting, gastronomically speaking, of all meals I have had at the Savoy.

It was an official luncheon given to the delegates attending an international Press Congress at the time. I happened to be a journalist then, among other things. I was the London correspondent of a Paris journal with the greatest circulation in France; it was called *La Croix* and every French parish priest was sent a gift copy. My '*Lettres de Londres*' were signed Jean Niquet, a pen name. The Savoy lunch was given with tables of twelve or sixteen, the delegates of each different country sitting together with one or two London members who could speak their language as hosts. I was, of course, given a table of French journalists to look after, with Mr. Wickham Steed, of *The Times*, who spoke French like a Frenchman, as co-host. The fare was the same for all, but at each table the host was expected to choose from the Savoy wine list the wine likely to please the guests at his table. Obviously I had to choose a French wine, and I did. I asked the sommelier, before the lunch, to decant six bottles of Château Laujac and put them on the table so that all could help themselves, which they did, and appeared to be quite satisfied. For many years Château Laujac has been the first and cheapest claret on the Savoy Wine list. It is a very charming property of the Cruse family in the Bas Médoc, an *ordinaire*, but fair enough *pour le soif* to drink and forget about it, not to write about. Quite good enough for the occasion. I was quite startled when my co-host lifted his glass, looked at me, and asked: ' *Quel est ce vin merveilleux?* ' What could I do? Tell the truth? I did! ' *C'est le numéro un sur la liste du Savoy.* ' He took No. 1 to be the best. If my friend took 'Number One' to mean the best wine on the list, why not let him? So I quickly became very much engaged with some argument with one of the French journalists!

Many are the happy memories I have of dinners in Vintners' Hall, either as the guest of one of the Members of the Court, or as host when the Saintsbury Club or the Wine and Food Society were graciously given leave to hold their dinners in the noble Hall. One dinner which stamped itself on my mind more forcibly than all others is the one and only unhappy dinner I had there. Its date had been fixed weeks or months before anyone could have dreamed of Edward VIII's abdication, and as it did not become known more than about one hour before the dinner was to be served, served it had to be; but when we all stood up to drink the Loyal Toast, we knew that there was no King. Edward was no longer King and his brother George did not become King before the next morning!

Gus Loring, Augustus Peabody Loring to give him his full name, was a true Bostonian, and a truly lovable person. He was benevolent and intelligent; he had a sense of humour and a sunny happy disposition. He was a wonderful host. I remember dining at his house in Boston, Mass., with him and his wife, and Charlie and Theodora Codman, Mrs. Philip Dexter and two other guests, eight in all: a very simple meal with a very good soup to begin with and a saddle of lamb as the main dish—but a saddle that made the meal memorable. It was placed before Gus, who rose and carved it expertly; when all were served, Gus sat down and the dish before him was taken away. A pleasant half hour passed as we talked about all sorts of things including the two fine red wines which Gus had decanted for us. Then the plates were taken away, a pile of hot plates were put before Gus and then another saddle of lamb which Gus rose to carve! 'What extravagance!' thought or said the guests. 'Not at all,' Gus quickly and smilingly told us: 'this second saddle was put in the oven half an hour after the first, and the second helping will be just as good as the first, which it could not have been otherwise. We have children, grandchildren and staff who will thoroughly enjoy cold saddle of lamb, and none of it will be wasted.'

Gus and his wife were often away from Boston, visiting or staying at their home by the sea, but the Boston house was never closed and any of their married children, if they came to Boston, knew that their old home was still their home. Gus had a fine cellar of wine in which the bins had either red, white or blue rosettes. Any of the children who happened to be in Boston in the absence of their parents, could take any wine from a red rosette bin, but not from a blue rosette bin unless they were entertaining a friend who really appreciated fine wine. On no account were they to take a bottle from a white rosette bin. These were the best wines, and they never did.

There is another dinner which I remember with no sense of guilt, but because I made the mistake of not keeping my mouth shut—how can anyone keep his mouth shut at table? It was a Burgundy dinner, given by Mr. and Mrs. Pereira in Boston, Mass., in 1935 or 1936, and I knew that we were to have four red Burgundies because my host had asked me to help him decant the four bottles. The food was very good and the service was rather too good—by which I mean too quick, so that we still had in our glasses some of the No. 3 Burgundy when a very creamy and rich-looking confection came to the table. Thinking of No. 4 Burgundy, the last and best, which was decanted and must be drunk, I committed the indiscretion of asking my hostess, next to whom I was sitting, if I could have a little cheese. 'Certainly not,' she snapped back at me in a tone which gave no hope of a change of heart—or of the woman having a heart at all—'You've had quite enough to eat.' That was that. And she was so right! She might even have added that I had had enough to drink. Anyhow, the unexpected rebuff certainly stamped the meal on my mind, making it memorable for ever.

Mrs. Pereira's 'No' to cheese reminds me of a Wine and Food Society's luncheon in London when a very ripe creamy whole Brie was passed round on its straw mat. As the lady next to me helped herself she asked the waiter for some butter and he brought it to her. When he had gone, I could not help asking her: 'Do you really think that so creamy a cheese needs any butter?' 'Of course not,' she replied somewhat tartly, 'I did not ask for butter for the cheese, but for the biscuit.' She certainly scored, and I could do nothing but apologize!

When *Tables of Content* was about to be published, Michael Sadleir told me that his firm would like him to entertain me and two friends of mine to a lunch, the venue, fare and wines of which they left to me, provided my two friends and I agreed to be photographed at table and to have our photo used by Constable as a jacket for my book. I asked my two best friends in the wine trade, Ian Campbell and Frances Berry, and both agreed to play, but as bad luck would have it, I chose the Trocadero, in Shaftesbury Avenue, as the restaurant for our lunch. Whatever the fare and wines were on that day I cannot remember: they were surely of the best. The Trocadero had in those days a famous chef, whom I knew well, and the finest cellar of wines in London. Yet all that I remember of that 'memorable meal' is the exasperation of us all as we sat on and on, long after we had finished our meal, waiting until every other customer had left the room before our photographer was allowed by the management to take our photo. It so happened that a short time before, a photograph had been published of some film star dining at the Trocadero, and in the dim distance, among diners at other tables, one could just recognize a man and a woman at a table for two: the woman happened to be the wife of a jealous husband, who brought forth the photo in his action for divorce, whilst the wife's boy friend brought an action for damages against Messrs. Lyons, who were not taking risks with photographers any more!

Some ten years earlier, when Sir Louis Bower was Lord Mayor of London and Monsieur de Fleuriau French

Ambassador, they were both my guests at a small luncheon party in a private room at the Ritz in London. My other two guests were Monsieur Raymond Poincaré, Prime Minister of France, and Cardinal Bourne, the then Archbishop of Westminster, who had really been the cause of this lunch: trained at St. Sulpice, Paris, and a sincere francophile like all the R.C. English priests of his generation, he regretted bitterly the impossibility of sending any of his young seminarists to France since the anti-clerical laws of Monsieur Combes; he had told my old friend Ernest Oldmeadow, who was then editor of *The Tablet* and in constant touch with the Cardinal, that he would very much like an opportunity of an informal meeting with the French Prime Minister during his visit to London; Oldmeadow told me, and Avignon, the Ritz chef, gave us, no doubt, a wonderful meal, but it was not the fare that made it a 'memorable meal'; it was the guests and the conversation.

Oldmeadow's name brings back to my memory two occasions when he was the host: a lunch in the top room of his Dean Street Office, when he was both host and cook, and a dinner at the Richelieu, at the corner of Dean Street and Oxford Street. The luncheon party was a very small one and a very odd one; I never understood why Oldmeadow had asked me to be there; his other two guests were Monsignor Godfrey, Papal legate at the time, who became Cardinal and Archbishop of Westminster later; and Hore Belisha, who was no longer the Transport Minister but still a Jew—a Jew, however, who was thinking very seriously of becoming a Christian. The dinner party at the Richelieu was a much more jovial occasion with a truly comic sequel. Ernest and Cecilia Oldmeadow were hosts and two of their guests, besides my wife and myself, were Louis Meyniac, the senior partner of Messrs. Mestrezat, Meyniac, of Bordeaux, and his niece, Mademoiselle Dussau, who was no little girl but an elderly spinster. She had been governess to the children of Lord Tennyson, who happened to be Governor of Australia when King George V paid an official visit to the country and, evidently on Lord Tennyson's recommendation, engaged Mademoiselle Dussau as Princess Mary's French tutor. So, after dinner, the uncle had to see his niece safely back to the Palace. A taxi was called and Meyniac, with a wave of the hand, told the driver to go to Buckingham Palace. The taxi driver was not too sure and asked: 'D'ye mean Buckingham Palace Hotel?' There was then such a hotel in Buckingham Palace Road which has since become offices for the I.C.I. 'Of course NOT,' shouted Meyniac, 'I mean Buckingham Palace, where the King lives, and I am Louis Meyniac.' That last piece of information was unnecessary and unfortunate. 'Get out of my cab,' growled the driver, 'I'll have none of your sort.' Rude or not, my wife and I could not help a good laugh as we took Meyniac's taxi to drive us to Carlisle Place, next to the Victoria Palace.

There is a meal which I have remembered for the last thirty years with a slightly uneasy sense of guilt. Jacques Cartier, a dear friend of mine who died much too young, had asked me to lunch with him at the Savoy, in June 1934, and had asked me to see if I could devise a menu that would be different from anything his other three guests had ever had before; his other three guests were the first Lord Rothermere, Sir Henry Deterding, and Sir John Sutton, all rich men used to the best of everything. The food, which I settled with Francis Latry, was both excellent and unusual: a Risotto of Ecrevisses as Entrée; grilled Turtle Fins with a Beurre Blanc for the main course; a large Aubergine stuffed with Mushrooms as an Entremets de Légumes. A ripe peach with the first raspberries and a Crème d'Ananas as dessert. A wonderful meal, indeed, and those three rich men praised it unanimously, they also liked the wine very much, but they could not actually 'place' it; it was a wine the like of which they had never tasted before, and would never taste again: it was, I told them, a wine not to be had from any of the London wine-merchants. It was a blend of my own, a bottle of 1929 still Champagne and a bottle of 1929 Zeltinger! Quite unorthodox, no doubt: a trick, I admit, but not a fraud—at least I hope not.

Exceptions apart, however, Memorable Meals are meals of outstanding interest and excellence according to the standard of the age, and the standard of gastronomy of the pre-World War I age was very different from what it has been since.

Food was better in those days because it was fresher, but you did not expect, nor did you want, anything that was not in season. More important is the fact that food was also very much cheaper than it has been ever since: we had little money then and yet managed to have a good table and five well-fed, happy, healthy children. Wine also was both better and cheaper than it has ever been since; better because there were still quite a number of pre-phylloxera wines to be had at reasonable prices, and cheaper because there had been an unprecedented sequence of fine vintages, in France and Germany; also there was a glut of very nice wines at ridiculously low prices. Last, but by no means least, the men, women and children of the pre-World War I age were certainly different from the men, women and children who are as young today as we were then. Whether we were better or worse physically, intellectually, morally, or otherwise, I cannot say, but it is quite easy to prove beyond all argument that we had appetites and digestive organs far superior to those of the present time. Menus of the time prove it; here is, for instance, the menu of a business lunch in my office, at 24 Mark Lane, when five of my business friends joined me for lunch:

The Fare: Tortue claire
        Omelette aux Fines Herbes
        Sole grillée
        Poulet Reine, Pommes sautées
        Fromage

The Wines: Pommery & Greno 1889
    Château Margaux 1877
    Château Branaire-Ducru 1877
    Château Mouton-Rothschild 1877
    Château Lafite 1878
    Château Léoville-Poyferré 1874
    Château Langoa-Barton 1875, Magnum
    Hine's Grande Champagne 1834

Six Clarets for six of us, a bottle apiece, was considered quite normal then. The date of that lunch was 17 March 1907, a few days after my thirtieth birthday. Of course, I could not eat so much food today, being over ninety, although I might enjoy the same number of wines if only they were still available. But there are no young people in their thirties today who would and could sit down to such a meal and enjoy it as thoroughly as we did in 1907.

There is a meal for which I was responsible, which is why I remember it, although I did not attend it. I think that it is entitled to a place here. Gerald Kelly and I first met at the hospitable board of my old friend Francis Berry at Wimbledon in 1929 or 1930. He was my guest for lunch at 24 Mark Lane, and we dined together a number of times at Park Row, with Guy Knowles who left, at his death, the wines that were in his cellar to Kelly. Both Guy Knowles and Gerald Kelly were early members of the Saintsbury Club. When Sir Gerald Kelly became President of the Royal Academy in 1949 or 1950, he came to see me and told me that he had had to put up with a dreary meal year after year, at Burlington House, and there was nothing he could do about it. But now he was the boss, and he wanted the annual Banquet to be a really good meal. How could it be done was the question he came to ask me. I told him that a fine meal was out of the question, since there were no kitchens at Burlington House, and the caterers had to bring the food in containers from the City to Piccadilly; all I could suggest for what would be a good meal, would be to start

G

with a turtle soup, telling the caterers that it must be served very hot, and they must give plenty to everybody. Served with it, an old Sercial Madeira in glasses of sensible size, not miniature so-called Sherry glasses.

Then Scotch Salmon and plenty of Champagne. As main dish, cold ribs of the finest Beef, underdone, and potatoes in their jackets. A good, fairly old but not too old Claret. Finish with a really first class, just ripe, Stilton and an old Port, also served in glasses of sensible size, not the usual little bastard Port glasses. When I saw Kelly, a little after the banquet, and asked him whether it had been a success or a failure, he said 'Failure' without hesitation; 'the members were furious at their annual banquet being made a kind of picnic.' 'But,' he added, 'there was only one man there who, like myself, thoroughly enjoyed, for the first time, a meal at Burlington House; he was not an R.A. He was a guest—Winston Churchill.'

When I first came from Reims to Pommery's London office, at 24 Mark Lane, I was sent by my firm, each spring, to visit some of our old and valued customers, give them as best I could the right answers to any questions they asked me about Champagne, what the last vintage promised to give us, or when our next vintage Cuvée would be offered. It was, of course, a more polite age than the present, and before going to Yorkshire or any part of the country, I would write to the few firms who were old clients, and ask which day would suit them to see me. The usual reply was a choice of two or three days, and an invitation to dine and stay the night on the chosen day. I never forgot my one and only *tête-à-tête* dinner with old Mr. Fennell. After a very fine meal, the table was cleared and two beautiful decanters full of wine were placed on the shining mahogany table in front of the old gentleman, who asked me a question which nearly made me fall off my chair: 'Will you have Port or Claret?' Of course, I said Port, and my host gave me the name of the shipper and the date of the vintage—something like Cockburn 1847, but I am not sure. I was not told what the Claret was by my host, and I did not want to show that I had never heard that Claret could be an after-dinner wine especially as he was drinking Claret when I was drinking an incomparable Port. I was told later that old Fennell was probably drinking that evening his own Claret in every sense of the word, a good enough Margaux or Pauillac but somewhat light, and he had made a far better wine of it, in his own opinion, by blending it with a fine red Hermitage, with both body and age! It may well have been the case. I have had an invoice of the mid-nineteenth century from Thomson, of Leith, quite clearly describing the invoiced Bordeaux as 'hermitaged'. That was long before anybody had thought of the *Appellations contrôlées*!

It does not seem right to me somehow to end this collection of odd memorable meals on one over sixty-five years old. True as it is that I have lost most of my old friends, I have had the privilege to make new friends in my old age and I would like the last of all those odd memorable meals to be that which took place only two years ago, when both fare and wines were memorable in their own right, but the company and the occasion were even more memorable.

The name of this particular friend of mine was Rhodes, an American doctor, not the sort who gives you something nasty to drink when you have a cough, but a scientist research doctor who came to Oxford with his wife nearly every year for a few days, and I usually had dinner with them, in London, either when on their way to or from Oxford.

In March 1967, I had a letter from Dr. Rhodes giving the dates of his visits to London and Oxford, in May, with his wife, when they hoped to see me. I wrote to him and told him how sorry I was about it but I was very much afraid

that I would be unable to see them in May as my London
lease came to an end in March, after twenty-one years, and
I had decided to leave London and end my days at Little
Hedgecourt, near East Grinstead, which had been our
summer place for some fifty years; it had been for some
time the home of my eldest son and his family, and it
would henceforth be my home as well. I added that
knowing as I did how precious his time was, I dare not ask
him and his wife to come to Little Hedgecourt for lunch,
happy as I would be to see them, but the London–East
Grinstead train service was so bad.

I heard no more about it. There was nothing else to be
done or said. So I thought, but I was wrong. At the end of
April or the first days of May, I had another letter from
Dr. Rhodes. He informed me that after receiving my last
letter he had made inquiries and learnt that there was
near East Grinstead, hence not far from Little Hedgecourt,
a place called Gravetye Manor, where the food and the
wines were very good. So he would come with his wife, by
car, on 17 May at 12.30 to collect me, my son and his wife
and all go to Gravetye Manor for lunch. He added that he
had asked his friend, and my friend, Otto Loeb, in London,
to attend to the menu, the wines and all details.

On 17 May, at 12.30, Dr. and Mrs. Rhodes arrived at
Little Hedgecourt according to plan, collected me, my
daughter-in-law and my daughter Jeanne in place of her
brother who happened to be abroad.

We were soon at Gravetye Manor which, of course, I
have known for many years, and we were met by Otto
Loeb who did not lead us to the dining room and a table
for six but to a sitting room where we presently sat down
to a beautifully laid table for twelve. Besides the six of us,
there were Dr. and Mrs. Dickerson, Dr. and Mrs. Adamson,
Dr. Knudsen, whom I had known longer than any of the
others, Otto Loeb and Johnny Avery. All but the last two
had just flown from the States into London.

What a compliment! What a privilege! So undeserved!

Loeb's commissariat had been wonderful. I remember that the two main dishes were Salmon and roast ribs of Beef, both perfect. Of all the wines the Magnum of Château Latour 1929 stood out as supreme.

This may be the last but surely not the least of the memorable meals I remember in the twilight.

XII. GASTRONOMES, GOURMANDS
and GOURMETS

GASTRONOMY owes its name to Gaster, the most important part of our anatomy. We may be sound of brain, heart and lungs, but only so long as Gaster—the belly—keeps the whole of our inner self working properly, and this it cannot do if we are mean or stupid—if we do not give it enough food, or the right kind of food. In the bad old days, the rich ate too much and drank too much while the poor ate too little—but still drank too much.

Dr. Johnson loved his food and brandy, but he was no gastronome. There is no 'gastronomy' in his Dictionary. It was only during the Victorian age, when serious efforts were made to check excessive drinking at all social levels, that *Gastronomie* was accepted in England and in English as Gastronomy. Gastronomy means the intelligent choice and appreciation of whatever is best in food and drink for Gaster the belly, as well as a lively sensual satisfaction to our sense and sight, smell and taste. There cannot be any intelligent choice nor real appreciation where there is excess. Gastronomy stands or falls by moderation. No gourmand and no glutton can be a gastronome. No hard drinker can be a gastronome. His taste-buds get blurred and seared by alcohol. Of course, there are gastronomes who are extravagant and who spend more than they should to have the best, just as there are motorists who buy cars beyond their means. But wealth is no more indispensable to be a gastronome than to be a motorist. What is quite indispensable is to be born with good senses of smell and taste, gifts that no money can buy. Some people are born colour blind, and others are born with a defective or no sense of smell or taste. The great Duke of Wellington, for instance, could not tell beef from mutton or pork—he had no taste and he knew it. But he insisted on having a good chef for the sake of his friends.

But whilst the blind cannot pretend to see, nor the deaf pretend to hear, the man and woman with no sense of smell or taste, or poor defective ones, may pose as connoisseurs, and sometimes do. I could name a few, but I had better not. What I can record, many years ago however, is having a bet with Stephen Walter, the younger brother of John, of *The Times*, when dining at his London flat. He had excellent senses of smell and taste, and knew a good deal about wine. He was responsible for the first Wine Supplement ever published by *The Times*, in June 1914. I bet that he could not taste wine from water by taste alone, with a napkin over his eyes. We filled three glasses, all exactly the same of course, with Sherry, Port, and water, and gave him Port and Sherry to sip and sip again, and he named them correctly. Then we gave him the glass of water, and without any hesitation he said 'Sherry again'. Off came the napkin over his eyes and he was left staring at the glass of water in his hand! It made us laugh, but it did not make any difference to our opinion that he was a good judge of wine under normal conditions.

Is Gastronomy really necessary? Yes and No. Yes in England, France and highly civilized nations with a high standard of living, but No elsewhere. A high standard of living depends upon both the quantity and quality of available food and drink, and there is no difficulty in the right measuring of quantity in tons or ounces, yards and inches, not enough or too much. But who and where are the people we can trust to tell what is bad, good or indifferent, what is best and the next best? There is no yardstick for quality and nobody can reasonably expect anything but praise, deserved or not, from the salesman for whatever he has to sell. That is why Gastronomy is necessary. The gastronome knows what is best and demands the best in both food and drink. The best is not necessarily the dearest; it is not the cheapest as a rule either, although it may be accidentally so. The true gastronome can definitely tell us what is the best. That is a fact; the best value is a matter of personal opinion; a matter of taste and circumstance, two greatly varying factors. Without gastronomes, without people who know and who care for the best, quality would soon go down to the level of what pays the seller best to sell.

Eustace Hoare was the model and pattern of a gastronome of my children's generation. He was the most generous host with always a gracious welcome for all, which is rather uncommon among such wealthy people as he was. His taste was exquisite and catholic. It was not only his food and wine that were of the best, but his pictures, glassware, silver and furniture. Everything he lived with had beauty and harmony. He was introduced to me in 1936, by C. M. Wells who had been his housemaster at Eton years before, as a suitable recruit for the Saintsbury Club. Suitable was hardly the right word—highly desirable would have been better, and although Eustace Hoare did not become a member before 1937, it was not long before he became a member of the small Committee of the Club, of which I was Chairman, during the first thirty years of the Club's existence, as well as Cellarer. Eustace Hoare was born in 1899, a great Claret year, as was also 1900, and for many years he loved to give his friends some of the first growths of both vintages and ask us which was the better of the two. We never could be quite sure; we never wished to be, both were so good! So there had to be another date and another dinner. Old age had no chance to spoil his good looks—he died much too young.

Two real gastronomes of my own generation—both a little older than myself, whom I knew for some thirty years, were Frederick and Percy Thellusson, who died as the 6th and 7th Lord Rendlesham. The first Lord Rendlesham's father was a Frenchman, born in Paris in 1737. He came to England in 1763, was naturalized English and made a great fortune as a merchant banker; he died in July 1797, at Plaistow, a fashionable residential place at the time, within a horseride of London. If he had had his wish, Frederick and Percy Thellusson's father would have been the wealthiest man in England. By the will which he made in 1796, he left a very large sum of money and real estate to accumulate during the life time of his sons and grandsons and to be divided at the death of the last grandson among the three eldest of his great-grandsons. Little as he knew it, the lawyer who drew up that will enriched three generations of London lawyers. Litigation began as soon as the testator had been laid to rest. The children wanted to have the will set aside, but failed and it went on until the House of Lords gave the final verdict at the end of the century. When the last of the testator's grandsons died, in 1856, there were then two claimants left, and the 5th Baron Rendlesham was one of them. (The first Baron was the Frenchman's eldest son, created in 1806.) The 5th Lord Rendlesham had three sons, Frederick, Percy and Hugh, who had been brought up in the lap of luxury as the sons of the man soon to be the richest man in the land, but by the time they were fully grown it became evident that they would have to do something for their living. Their father was by no means a poor man, but he had many financial responsibilities besides far too large a house. So Hugh went into the Army and his two elder brothers joined the firm of Burne, Turner and became wine-merchants. Mr. Burne was born in Brighton in the early eighteen-twenties and came to London—by coach, of course—in 1840 to be apprenticed at Allnuts, one of the older City wine-merchants. Eventually he started on his own as a wine-merchant and sold some of the best wines and Brandy. He was so old-fashioned that he refused to sell Whisky and Gin, the stuff that no gentleman ever drank.

But when he took a partner, a Mr. Turner, he was told
that all the most highly respected wine-merchants of
London did sell Whisky, so he agreed that Turner could
do so also. In 1900, however, Frederick left Burne, Turner
to join Lucien Loffet as agent for Pommery Champagne
and, when Lucien Loffet retired, I became Frederick's
junior partner until his father's death. When Frederick
became 6th Lord Rendlesham he left the City and Percy
joined me. Both knew what was best, and would have
nothing else. Frederick was, I think, the better judge and he
had a better wine memory. Percy was more articulate and
the better host. He wrote to me once about his new
britches, probably the Eton spelling for breeches, but he
never wrote 'Château O'Brien' for 'Haut Brion' as
Maurice Healy used to—for fun of course. In the summer of
1926 Colonel Hugh Thellusson came home on leave, from
India, and first went to Cornwall to stay for a few days with
his eldest brother, Frederick. He had the mischance to
catch a chill, which turned to pneumonia, and he died.
In August 1926, Frederick had to come to London and had
lunch at 24 Mark Lane with his brother Percy and myself.
It was the last time that I saw him. It was a very hot day,
indeed, and we had our traditional three bottles of Champagne: it was Frederick who had made it a tradition.
When a bottle was open and he approved of it after tasting,
it became *his* bottle. Other bottles could be opened and
tasted for other guests, but he was not interested; all he
asked for was to be left *his* bottle to himself. So Percy and
I did the same and it was more than enough for us both on
such a hot day. But not for Frederick, who suggested a
bottle of Vintage Port, and when we both quite firmly
refused, he turned to Baker, our faithful cellarman, and
asked for a pint of his own Port, not Port that he had made,
but that Cockburn had made for him for years—their
finest tawny wine with a dash of young vintage just before
bottling. As Baker went to get this wine, Frederick shook

his head rather sadly and mumbled audibly: 'Degenerates, degenerates, both of you, beaten by the weather'—then he drank his pint of Port. With coffee and cigars we had a marvellous Hine 1844 and Frederick said to his brother: 'You know, Percy, when Hughie came to stay with me, I asked him what he would like best. He said that he could get Champagne anywhere, but old Claret nowhere. So I gave him my last bottle of Latour 1875 and my last bottle of Lafite 1864.' And then he added, with what really sounded like sobs—'dear Hughie is gone, and my old Claret is gone!'

Both Frederick and Percy were large eaters, but they were not gourmands; they were gourmets with Victorian appetites. Gourmands and gluttons must have much or too much, but they are not really interested in quality. Gourmets, on the contrary, demand, know and appreciate that which is best, a little or a great deal of it according to their appetite. My dear wife, for instance, and her friend the Dowager Lady Swaythling, were both *petites* and hardly ate anything at all, but what they did eat had to be the best. As a matter of plain logic there is no reason why a gourmet, that is one who knows, demands and thoroughly appreciates that which is best, may not be a gourmand as well, so long as he wants a lot, but all of it of the best. I knew a man who could easily have qualified for both titles of gourmet and gourmand; Valentine, Lord Castlerosse. He was a very big man and his appetite was not Edwardian, it was gargantuan! I believe that he could easily have eaten solo a whole leg of lamb, bar the bone: yet he was no glutton!

I may as well confess that the real reason I never would have called Valentine a glutton was because I knew only too well that I was born a gourmand and became a gourmet! I have never forgotten what I believe to be my own original sin. If not the first *péché de gourmandise* of my life, it is the first which I remember with, of course, a right sense of guilt. I suppose that I must have been seven or thereabouts, that is when a boy reaches the age of reason. Louis Mousset, a friend of my father, came to dinner at rue Coetlogon, and brought as his contribution to the feast a wonderful *dessert*, the like of which I had never seen before—or since. It was a large tortoise-like cake, its shell made of *Moka* with dark ribs of *Chocolat*. It had four little dark legs and a little head also made of *Chocolat*. I had sneaked into the dining-room before dinner and nobody was there at the time. I had a close view of the Tortoise on the dresser, and was simply lost in admiration. Having reached the age of reason, unfortunately for the Tortoise, I remembered that a Tortoise was a shy animal and that it did not usually stick its neck out, and before I knew what had happened, its head had come off quite easily between my forefinger and thumb. It was simply delicious; I knew that it was wrong, but I could not resist the temptation: the four little legs of the Tortoise followed its head, and I sneaked out of the dining room before having been seen. When dessert time came that evening, the Tortoise was placed on the table to be cut and served, but it looked more like a football than a Tortoise. Then Mousset, the giver, said timidly: 'It was supposed to be a Tortoise and it had a head and legs, but they are not there any longer.' There were six of us boys round the table, but five of them were pink and one, greedy me, of course, scarlet. So I was sent to bed *sans dessert*!

Sheer greed of this kind is without any excuse whatsoever, but there have been occasions in my long life when I must have passed as a greedy fellow quite unfairly by people who did not realize that I had a very healthy appetite. I remember, for instance, the only time in my business career when I called upon a firm of distillers and wine-merchants at Coleraine, in Northern Ireland, and then proceeded to Londonderry, where I did not arrive until nearly 2 p.m. I was very hungry and went to the Station

Hotel at once for food—any food, hot or cold, would have been most acceptable. Much to my surprise, the young girl who had come to ask me what I wanted as I sat down at the first table by the door, in an empty dining room, came back almost instantly with a hot roast chicken which she placed before me. I cut it in two, as if it had been a pigeon, and having eaten the first half, I ate the other without any effort or any sense of guilt. Then the young girl came back, but it was too late; she looked very unhappy and I thought that she was going to burst into tears—as well she might have done! The chicken, it appeared, was meant to be the inn-keeper's family dinner, and they had given the visitor a chance to help himself first, a risk that they surely never took again.

One bright, frosty noonday—it must have been in 1904 or 1905—Toby Folks and I happened to meet in the Strand, outside Romano's: we both had wished to see Luigi Naintré, but he was not in. 'Let's go and see old Mrs. O'Brien,' said Toby, adding, 'if you stand a bottle of Bollinger, I'll stand the oysters.' 'Done,' I promptly agreed, and up the little passage connecting the Strand and Maiden Lane we marched, arm in arm. Mrs. O'Brien was a raven-haired, eagle-eyed Irish woman who was in charge of the main ground floor room at Rule's in Maiden Lane. 'We'll have a bottle of Bollinger, please,' I said to Mrs. O'Brien, after the usual greetings. She looked at me hesitatingly; she had never known me to order any other wine than Pommery. Toby was jubilant and said to Mrs. O'Brien: 'Yes, it is quite in order—he wants to taste really fine Champagne for a change!' Then he added: 'The oysters are on me; I'll have a dozen best Whitstable!' 'And I'll have a hundred of the best Whitstable, please,' I said in the most casual manner. Toby yelped: 'Help! This is daylight robbery.' I pointed out to him that the offer to stand oysters—no limits mentioned—had been his own, and he really had no right to make such a fuss because

I happened to like oysters. All the same, to console him, I cut my order down to a mere eight dozen.

There was a time when oysters were a shilling a dozen; men would eat a hundred, and boys fifty—or half a hundred as they were called, without any fuss. But at half a crown per oyster, the price of the best Colchesters today, an oyster feast has become well-nigh immoral.

XIII. WITHOUT PREJUDICE

THERE is sugar and there is Rum from a number of West Indian islands just as good as Cuba's sugar and Rum, but there are no cigars comparable in excellence to Havana cigars made in Cuba from Cuba-grown tobacco. Unfortunately, the people of Cuba are somewhat temperamental and there came a time, soon after the end of World War I, when the American firms engaged in the Havana cigar business lost their patience: they built a most scientifically equipped factory at Trenton, in New Jersey, and they had the freshly gathered tobacco leaves flown from Cuba to Trenton, there to be made into perfect cigars by dependable labour and under the intelligent supervision of experts. Somehow or other something must have gone wrong, because those Trenton-made cigars never were the same as the Havana-made ones: they looked exactly the same in the box, but they were not nearly so good to smoke. At any rate, rightly or wrongly, I did not like them. It did not really matter to me, since I could most easily carry my own Havana-rolled Santa Damianas—my favourite brand—in my cigar case, and this is what I did—much to Désiré's grief.

What the Trenton people did or paid for the privilege, I neither knew nor cared, but there were no cigars for sale at the time other than Trenton-made brands at any of the Savoy group hotels. Désiré was then sommelier at the Savoy, one of the best of men and of head-waiters: I was very fond of him, but not to the point of buying from him Trenton cigars. One day, lunching at the Savoy with a friend, and both of us smoking a Santa Damiana from my case, after lunch, Désiré handed to me a beautiful great cigar which he asked me to accept with the management's compliments and to smoke 'without prejudice'. He was sure that if I would only do so, I would realize that, although from Trenton, this cigar was exactly the same as if made at Havana. I promised to do my best to oblige.

That same evening, we happened to be alone at home, after dinner, my wife and I, and I never thought of saying anything to her about Désiré's cigar, which I started smoking with every intention of liking it if I could. But, of course, I did know that it was a Trenton cigar. My wife knew absolutely nothing about it, yet it was not long before she turned up her little nose and said to me: 'What are you smoking? It cannot be one of your cigars.' 'You are absolutely right, my dear,' I told her; 'and you and I will lunch at the Savoy tomorrow, and I would like you to tell Désiré just what has happened. He asked me to smoke this cigar without prejudice: I could not do so since I knew what it was, but you did not, and you very quickly found that there was something different about it—without prejudice.'

And so the next day to the Savoy for lunch. When Désiré heard what had happened, it made him so miserable that I had to order a double brandy to cheer him up. And they still had the Denis Mounié 1865 in those days!

My dear wife had a much keener sense of smell than I have. On several occasions she detected the faintest trace of corkiness in a wine just opened, which I did not smell until the wine had been in the glass for a while, but there was once a British Consul in Rosario, in N. Argentina, whose name was Noel and who would tell his friends that André Simon could tell, after a few whiffs, the name of the brand of any cigar anyone happened to be smoking. Of course, I never could do anything of the sort, and never pretended that I could, but Noel's belief in my wonderful sense of smell was due entirely to a piece of luck I had when he and I were passengers in 1907 from Santos to Buenos Aires on the good ship *Thames*, one of the oldest of the Royal Mail

Steamship Company's fleet. She was really a cargo ship but carried a few passengers at a lower rate of fares. When I went for the first time to South America on business in 1907, I landed first at Rio de Janeiro where I spent a little time before proceeding by train to São Paolo. When I had been there long enough the *Thames* called at Santos on her way to Buenos Aires and it was much better for me to take my passage by *Thames* rather than wait another week at São Paulo for the mail boat. We were only eight or ten passengers and we all had dinner together with the ship's captain. At the end of the meal, no memorable meal, the man next to me, whose name I did not know, took out of his pocket, a cigar case, and out of it a cigar which was tightly wrapped up in several pieces of silver paper to protect it from the damp sea air. It had no band. Then he lit it with due care and started smoking, it did smell good, very good, and how I would have loved to have had such a cigar to smoke! I had left Southampton with a few Santa Damiana cigars, my favourite brand, the only brand I knew, in fact, and I only knew it because it was the brand which Frederick Thellusson smoked and he had given me a box. So in sheer desperation, I said to the man with the cigar: 'How lucky you are to have a Santa Damiana to smoke.' By an extraordinary piece of luck it was a Santa Damiana that he was smoking, and from that evening until we reached, rather too soon, Buenos Aires, I smoked a Santa Damiana cigar in the evening with Mr. Noel who was on his way to Rosario as British Consul.

Some twenty years later, after World War I, when I could afford to buy good cigars and enjoy one after lunch and one after dinner, but no more, the Prince of Wales went on a goodwill tour of the Empire on board H.M.S. *Renown*. When the ship left Jamaica, the cigar people of the island presented the Prince with a box of large and beautiful cigars. He must certainly have thanked them warmly but, as he never smoked cigars, he gave the box to

H

an officer on *Renown*, a non-smoker, and when the *Renown* returned to England, he gave that box of great cigars to my old and very dear friend, Ian M. Campbell, also a non-smoker. He knew that Ian was a non-smoker, but he also knew that I did smoke cigars and they were given to Ian for me. They still looked beautiful but no care had been taken on board and the inside leaves were white with mould. Absolutely unsmokable! What a tragedy!

Another twenty years went by and we had another war. No more cigars from Havana for the duration. Cigar prices went up and my income went down, so fate had made up my mind for me to give up cigars, but it was not to be. I received one day in 1941 a short note from the London Office of the Orient Line asking me to call and see Mr. X who had a parcel for me from Australia. The parcel had reached London in some curious way about which I had no wish to make any fuss, and it was made up of four boxes each containing twenty-five big Hoyo de Monterey cigars. They were a gift from the most generous of all the friends I have ever had, Jim McGregor of Sydney. I wrote to him and thanked him, of course, but added, 'please, do not do it again. There is nothing I can send you or do for you, and it is not fair.' But he did do it again and again after writing to me, 'Do not be an ass. Those cigars are not sent to you but to your dear wife. You must know that I love her and I know that she loves the smell of a good cigar. All you have to do is to smoke them and give her some pleasure with my love. Jim.' P.S. Jim's cigars were not contraband; they bore the Customs duty. I do not know how it was done, but I imagine that the cigars came in the purser's locker and that the purser was also given the money to pay the duty.

XIV. WORLD WAR II

THERE must be somewhere in the brain some kind of jungle of faces and places out of which dreams are made without rhyme or reason; who knows? But where does memory store for a lifetime what we happen to have seen or heard? And how and why does memory choose to bring forth, unasked, old records out of storage? Who knows? I was trying to remember what happened to us during World War II, some thirty years ago, when memory brought before me quite clearly an old man with a red face all dressed in red whom I recognized at once as Cardinal Richard, Archbishop of Paris, not thirty but eighty years ago. He was sitting in an armchair in the middle of the front row, watching the performance of one of the tragedies of Euripides, all in the original Greek, by boys of the Petit Séminaire Notre Dame des Champs, where I was a boarder. I never understood a single word of the play, but the cardinal, the stage, and the scene were evidently registered by memory. I learnt Greek later, and forgot it, remembering only that the tragedies of Euripides started with a Prologue, when two choirs, on the right and left of the stage, sang or told to each other that something dreadful was sure to happen; then came blue murder when the play proper did start; then came the Epilogue, when the same two choirs started again singing or saying to each other: 'Didn't I tell you?'

Whether I was half asleep and dreaming at the time or not, World War II came before me as one of the tragedies of Euripides, with what we called the phoney war, from September 1939 to May 1940, as the Prologue; then blue murder—four years of it—and finally the Epilogue from the liberation of France, in 1944, to the unconditional surrender, in 1945.

When war was declared, in September 1939, it seems to me today, when I am thirty years older and I have reached the age of reason, that my friend A. J. A. Symons and I, the Secretary and President of the Wine and Food Society, must have been disconcerted, desolated, distressed by what really amounted to a death sentence for our six-year-old venture. To preach the gospel of gastronomy in wartime was sheer folly, nor could we expect our Members to pay a subscription when there would be no luncheons, no dinners, and no tastings for them; not only was food rationed, but there was no more wine coming in and the wine-merchants did not part easily with stocks that they could not replace. I cannot understand how it happened, but I remember quite clearly that we were annoyed but by no means alarmed, let alone distressed. The September number of 1939 had just been posted to the Members, together with the Programme of the Society's functions during October, November and December, and, incredible as it sounds, they were all held on the due dates and largely attended. I then prepared the Programmes of functions that were to be held in London in January, February, March, and April 1940, as if the 1939 war would have been settled by then. Rationing did make things more difficult, of course, but by no means impossible. This is probably how and why A. J. A. Symons had a brain wave: his last, before he became so ill.

Every man, woman, and child in the land was given an official ration book, a small book with lots of coupons for all rationed foods to which they were entitled week by week. It was a nuisance, of course, to queue up at the butcher's and grocer's. Grocers were easy to get on with; they gave you whatever they were allowed to and cut off the whole or half the corresponding coupon; but some butchers were difficult; unless they liked your face or your manners they never had the kind or cut of meat that you happened to want, and you

had to be content with the right number of ounces to which
you were entitled given to you over the counter.

What I did not realize, and what I believe was not appreciated by people like ourselves who could afford to buy unrationed food, was that the ration book had been like manna
from heaven for millions of working-class families who had
managed to live for some years immediately before the war on
the dole—that is, very near starvation. Most teenagers had
never had a day's work or a square meal before or after
leaving school. War was a blessing! All who were fit enough
to be conscripted were now fed as never before, and all
others, the very old excepted, male and female, had work
and money to buy food, rationed or not.

The last brainwave of my poor friend A. J. A. Symons, who
little knew how soon he was to be the victim of the haemor-
rhage of the brain that killed him, was that he, and I, and
our friends might well be depressed by the national ration
book, forgetting that there was a far greater choice of excellent foods which were not rationed. So he decided that the
Society should bring out an Unration book, similar in size
and shape to the national ration book, but blue instead of
beige. The coupons, which were never to be cut off, had
numbers, and each one corresponded to a food or dish which
could be had without any difficulty, mostly fish, vegetables,
game, fruit and so on. It was no cookery book, of course, but
it did remind you that a herring, for instance, could be
boiled, fried, grilled, baked, soused, etc. each sort having
a coupon number of its own. The list of the unrationed foods
had been the work given to me to do by A.J. He was so sure
that the demand for the Unration Book would be immense,
that he would not listen to any suggestion that a million
copies was rather more than we could hope to sell right
away. He may well have been quite right and it is possible
that we would have sold a million copies in a single week.
But our wonder horse never reached the winning post
because it never started. A million copies of Unration Books

meant a lot of paper and a good deal of money, two essential
commodities which even A.J.'s wonderfully persuasive
eloquence failed to get.

Incredible as it seems to me now, although we had been
at war with Germany since September 1939, I flew to Paris
in April 1940 and took the train from Paris to Dreux,
according to the official time table: my brother Pierre met
me at Dreux station and drove me to his farm where my
aged mother was being looked after. I had come over to see
her for what I knew would be the last time. After lunch,
back to Dreux by car, to Paris by train and to London by
air. By one of the most extraordinary of all extraordinary
coincidences, I met in Paris Jacques Bollinger, of Ay, and
Charles Codman, of Boston, Mass., both so much younger
than me, yet both now gone.

It was in October 1939 that A. J. A. Symons became ill
and that I had to make 6 Little Russell Street my office and
carry on single handed the affairs of the Wine and Food
Society until the end of the phoney war. Besides rationed
foods, the only wartime measure which made things more
difficult was the blackout. But that only meant lunches
instead of dinners. In 1939, I remember a very good oysters
and venison luncheon at the Gargoyle Club; David Tennant
was there but I cannot remember who was his wife at the
time. The November Lunch was at the Waldorf, and the
Christmas Lunch at the Dorchester.

In spite of it all, many Members resigned in January
1940, but the functions we gave in January, February,
March, April, and May 1940 were well attended!

The two functions of 1940 which I remember are the
Scottish lunch, when my old friend Colonel Ian Maxwell
Campbell of Airds was in the Chair, with Mrs. Winston
Churchill, a Member of the Society at the time, on his right;
I sat on her right. Scotch salmon and haggis were not
rationed nor was venison. The other was a Burgundian
luncheon at the Langham Hotel, when Marius Dutrey,

who was the Chef and my friend, managed to give us somehow a meal that might be fairly called pre-war! I did not
inquire how it was done at the time, but I am glad to know
that Marius Dutrey is still my friend, although no longer
a Chef. I am quite sure that we had a Claret Dinner at the
Carlton, in March, I think, but I cannot remember how we
beat the black-out that evening, nor why I was not present
at either the April or May functions. I know that I asked
Sir Eric Maclagan, a Member of the Society's Advisory
Council, to take the Chair at an Oyster Festival in the Great
Hall of the Connaught Rooms; Kenward, George Harvey's
brother-in-law, who was in charge, told me later that there
were no oysters opened elsewhere that day in London as he
had all the professional oyster openers at the Connaught
Rooms.

Try and try again as I have done in the twilight to
remember why I was not at the May Meeting of the Society
I cannot remember, but I know that I had planned it as
an entirely vegetarian meal and that I had asked my dear
friend Sir Jack Drummond to take the Chair. We had by
then come to the end of the phoney war or Prologue; we
knew that we were in now for bloody war, but, happily,
we had no idea that we were to have four and a half
years of it!

We gave up our London flat: room had to be found somehow for furniture and books at Little Hedgecourt which
became our one and only residence for the duration of the
war, as well as the official address of the Wine and Food
Society.

We bought Little Hedgecourt in 1919. It was mostly very
poor land, 28½ acres of it, some waterlogged, most of it
choked by self-sown shrubs and trees of no quality whatsoever, besides brambles and weeds galore. It stretched
along the whole of the south shore of Hedgecourt pond
or lake, sixty acres of water twenty-eight miles S.S.W. of
Charing Cross as the crow flies. The whole of the waterside

was sheer watery jungle, but the opposite boundary of the land was the Surrey side of the Copthorne road, the boundary between Sussex and Surrey. No jungle there but two cottages, flowers and vegetables. The cottage nearer the road, but, happily, not by the roadside, must have been built at least 250 years ago. The owner from whom we bought it had done his best to modernize it, including a small bathroom; small, indeed, but quite large enough as the only water available was what was pumped from the well some distance outside. The other cottage was a late Victorian building some 500 yards farther away from the road. The chief attraction was the lake, and the next was the privacy; there was nobody between the lake and road, we had no fear of next door neighbours. So we added four bedrooms and two bathrooms to the old cottage, brought in the main water and electricity, and, in good time, turned the jungle into an ideal playground for our children and their friends. I was well off during the twenties and had five gardeners. The head gardener and his family lived in the Victorian cottage and Number 2 in a bungalow which I had built for him and his wife. We had two tennis courts, one hard and one grass, a bowling green, a putting green with a fairway approach to it and a bunker round it full of sea sand, an open air theatre and a seven-acre cricket field. Trees, rhododendrons and azaleas by the hundred. The dream of a tree lover and born gardener come true! But not for long! In 1933, when I had no money and no firm left, I still had Little Hedgecourt; I let it but did not sell it. In the summer of 1939, my wife and I were there alone and far from happy. We had hoped to spend our old age there with a host of grandchildren, maybe great-grandchildren, but two of our daughters were nuns in convents, one son was a Jesuit priest, and André, the eldest son, and Jeanne, the eldest daughter, were married, had a son each, lived their own lives and we saw little of them. Jeanne was at the time motoring on holiday with husband and son somewhere

on the Continent. So my wife and I had made up our minds
to sell Little Hedgecourt. It was not only too costly but too
depressing to be there by ourselves, with one gardener only,
Bill Serjeant, who did his best in the kitchen garden but had
no time for shrubs and flowers. When our agent told us that
he had a buyer willing to pay the price which we had asked
for, I asked him who and what he was: he was a house
builder who proposed to build a row of houses, complete
with garden and garage, from road to lake, after bulldozing
my lovely stretches of rhododendrons and azaleas. I could
not bear the thought of it and told the agent that the man
must pay one thousand pounds more than the original sum
demanded. He refused; he argued; his solicitor wrote. Then
war was declared and Little Hedgecourt was not sold. I cannot think what my wife and I would have done without
Little Hedgecourt during World War II. Indeed, we were
no longer alone. It was not long before meals had to be by
two sittings, usually the youngsters first and the elders next.
My dearly beloved daughter Jeanne had returned from the
Continent just in time, with husband, son and car. My wife
and I were only too happy to have them with us, when
they suggested coming for a few weeks, but that was thirty
years ago and I thank God every day to have her still with
me today. They never went back to London. Their Hamp-
stead house was badly damaged by a direct hit. Presently
they left Little Hedgecourt for the nearby Victorian cottage
which was my head gardener's home. They have since mod-
ernized it, not to say partly rebuilt it to their own taste. But
I am wandering from World War II. I must get back to it,
that is to May 1940, when we left London and settled at
Little Hedgecourt for the duration of the war.

Where was money, and food, let alone wine, to come
from ought to have had first priority, of course; but it came
only second. I am ashamed to say that I gave more time and
thought to the problem of keeping the Wine and Food
Society alive than to the feeding of my own people! Since

there was no possibility of giving the faithful few Members at home and many more overseas any functions that they could either attend or read about, the one and only way to give them an unquestionable proof that the Society was neither dead nor dormant was to send them four times a year, as before, their copy of *Wine and Food*, the Society's quarterly magazine. Could it be done? It was done. Every Member of the Society received his or her *Wine and Food* quarterly on the due dates during the war years and the difficult immediate post-war years when printing paper was so difficult to get. The friend who made this near miracle possible was my namesake, Oliver Simon, of The Curwen Press: he not only managed to get the necessary paper and to have the quarterly printed at The Curwen Press as long as it could be done, but when The Curwen Press was put out of action by a direct hit, he found a friendly competitor printer who printed our magazine for his sake, not mine. It is as a token of my gratitude to Oliver Simon and The Curwen Press that I have requested that this last book of mine, which I will never read, should be printed at The Curwen Press.

Paper was the major problem at the time, but not the only one. The Curwen Press had to be given something to print, and it was far from easy to find a suitable number of printable articles. I wonder whether I am right or unwise to make a confession? If one looks through the wartime numbers of *Wine and Food*, one will find that there are quite a number of articles written by authors whose names will not be found in Who's Who or anywhere else, but their first name is either Albert, Arthur, Archibald, Alan, Austin, invariably beginning with an A, whilst their second name begins also invariably with an L, and the third with an S. All were written by me but, of course, in very different styles. In war as in love all is fair!

My friend and partner, A. J. A. Symons, died in 1941, in his 42nd year; a great loss not only to his many friends but to English literature. He had not been able to attend to the conduct of the Wine and Food Society for the previous eighteen months, and there was absolutely nothing he could have done about it, ill as he was. I did not think that his death could possibly make any difference to the Society at the time. I was quite wrong. Among the Members of the Society who wrote to me to tell me how sorry they had been to hear of my friend's and the Secretary of the Society's death, one added that he would like to see me next time I happened to come to London. His name was Ben MacPeake and his address 30 Grosvenor Gardens. I did not know him. We had a motor bus from East Grinstead to Victoria five mornings each week, returning from Victoria rather early. There were still trains from and to Victoria and Brighton stopping at Horley, seven miles from Little Hedgecourt. It was not long before I made a date with Ben MacPeake and I was both astounded and delighted when he told me that his firm owned both 28 and 30 Grosvenor Gardens, made up as one internally; that he was holding the fort with a small staff, that there were many rooms unoccupied and unwanted, that I could have any one of them as an office for the Wine and Food Society, of which he was a Member, rent free for the duration of the war. What a gift! I missed the East Grinstead bus that day but took a train from Victoria to Horley, and I was so happy to have an office, at last, that I walked on air, so to speak, the seven miles to Little Hedgecourt. Nos. 28 and 30 Grosvenor Gardens were the headquarters of *Good Housekeeping*. The room I had as an office was the first-floor drawing-room in what had been the residence of an Ambassador who, in Victorian days, lived practically within call of Buckingham Palace. As it turned out I was no ordinary tenant of the National Magazine Company, who owned a number of glossy magazines; I was privileged to be helped by everyone from the hall-porter to the cook. Obviously I did my best for them in return for their help, and whenever any of them happened to be in doubt or difficulty, they were always welcome to look for what they wanted in the many books in the Society's library, or in my old head.

Having a London office made such a difference! The delivery of *Wine and Food* from Plaistow to East Grinstead had been quite a problem before, but Grosvenor Gardens was easy, besides which they lent me trestle tables and gave me a helping hand when the magazine had to be put in envelopes, franked and posted.

The peace of an office all to myself—I had neither secretary nor typist at the time—was a real blessing. I not only made good progress with the various sections of a *Concise Encyclopaedia of Gastronomy*, my major work during World War II, but I managed to publish some little one shilling booklets which proved to be very popular. I wrote the first: its title was *Soups, Salads, and Sauces*; it told the wartime housewife how to give a little more gastronomic attraction to the family daily meals at little more or no more cost at all. The next two booklets were written by my friend Ernest Oldmeadow, a particularly good amateur cook as well as an enthusiastic wine lover and fairly successful wine-merchant. The first of his booklets was *Potatoes: to know and to serve*, and the second *The Lilies of the kitchen: onions, leeks shallots, garlic, and chives*, not a breath-taking but a breath-giving booklet! The fourth booklet *No starch, no sugar* was written by me for the benefit of my diabetic friends and others, but more or less entirely from information given to me by Heudebert, a firm specializing in foods for diabetics. The fifth and the most original of those wartime booklets *United we cook; a comedy of conjugal cooking* was written by a gifted but unhappy friend of mine, Doris Lytton Toye, giving servantless wartime newly-weds practical hints on how to make cooking a hobby rather than a chore. There was to be a sixth booklet *Run, rabbit, run* by Ambrose Heath, but I received at the time a very unpleasantly worded letter from the Paper Control Board telling me that attention had been drawn to the fact that I appeared to be publishing books and booklets without having ever asked, let alone received, a permit from the Paper Control Board. I wrote a most humble letter of apology and promised not to do it again.

Of course, I did a great deal of work during World War II, and thoroughly enjoyed it, but I also had a great deal of recreation and distraction at Little Hedgecourt; gardening was both a joy and a tonic.

Much of the ground, especially at both ends of the property, had gone back to jungle, but we managed to keep the rhododendrons and azaleas clear of brambles and self-sown beeches. Our only gardener, Bill, who had come to us on being demobbed, in 1919, and stayed with us until he died, in 1968, gave all his time to the sorts of vegetables that were wanted in the kitchen for the table. I did not compete with him. I had neither the wish, nor the time, nor the physical strength to do so. I specialized in plants which the gardeners I knew in our part of the world had never grown or even heard of. One friend, named Millar, whom I liked very much, suffered from diabetes and I grew for him some scolymus, the aristocrat of the great thistle clan; there is no starch whatever in its long, white, fleshy root. By far the most successful of my gardening experiments was the stevia peruviana, a little plant which, according to its name, must have come from Peru. There were under its smallish, shining green leaves a number of microscopic hairs, according to the book, although I was never able to see them with a magnifying glass, but they must have been there and they acted somewhat like nettles do, although in a very different way. When one of the stevia leaves touched your tongue or taste buds, your mouth was full of sugar. My friend was delighted with it; it gave him great pleasure to taste sweetness and quite safely, of course, since it was his own sugar!

Another plant which none of my gardener friends had ever seen before was the Pamir Lettuce. I suppose that it must somehow have been a lettuce since they had given it the name, but it had nothing to do with any salad of that name I or anybody else had ever seen. It bolted at birth and bore three small, narrow, straight, miserable leaves on top of a small bamboo-like stem. You took no notice of the three leaves, but when the stem was about two and a half or maybe three foot, cut it down or pulled the lot out of the ground; it was an annual, you did not eat the stem like an asparagus, but you boiled it, then slit it and ate a sort of grey marrow from it spread on warm toast. It was eatable, but not worth all the trouble it gave to prepare. The pokeweed or Phytolacca from seeds I had brought from Maryland was a far better investment; its many shoots, in the spring, were excellent hot or cold, like asparagus.

In the summer of 1941 or 1942 I had an example of how war secrets are kept sacred in wartime. Two men came to Little Hedgecourt from the War Office to inform me that our lake was going to be drained that night. They said that the sixty acres of water of Hedgecourt Pond, thirty miles or so due south south west of London, were too good a landmark —or water mark—especially on bright moonlit nights. I told them that the lake did not belong to me, but that did not matter; obviously the War Office in wartime could do what they thought best. What does matter, I added, is that when the sluice gates are broken the people on the Lingfield side of the main London road might have to be warned of the coming flood. That could not be done: nobody must know in case the Germans were told that their landmark had gone. I then told them that the bottom of the lake was not rock but mud and that wet mud and water puddles all over would shine in the moonlight very little less, if any less at all, than fathoms of water. They agreed that it might be so, but orders were orders. They went away. They had not been gone long when my phone rang. Mr. Sam Isaacs, or some such name, just wanted to let me know that he would be presently at the sluice end of the lake with his car and enough nets to catch all 'my' fish; he would be glad to give me some of the catch!

In 1944, after the liberation of France, I decided that there was no need to wait for the unconditional surrender of Germany, after Italy's, to give to the limited number of faithful Members of the Wine and Food Society the Victory Meeting promised to them in May 1940. There was still some fighting going on somewhere, I knew, but the war was won; victory was no longer in question. Now was the time for the Epilogue when the choirs of Euripides said or sang their last piece.

If the Wine and Food Society meant to make its existence or survival known to the world, its Victory Banquet had to be an unqualified success to be reported in the right way by the Press. How could it be done? Although there were not a great many Members left, those who would come to the Society's Victory Meeting would expect it to be quite an occasion and would most likely ask a number of friends as their guests, which, as a matter of fact, they did, as I had hoped they would, and many of them became Members. It meant having a large room, and I knew that I could not do any better than the Connaught Rooms, as I could count with all confidence upon Kenward doing his best for us. That was easy. All else was difficult. A good meal was unthinkable: the Ministry of Food did not allow us to pay more than five shillings for food, and not more than three courses without bread: bread counted as a course. The Ministry allowed us as much wine as we cared to buy from them, mostly Algerian and some Italian wines that were not at all good. One could still get a bottle of good wine if one happened to know one of the few wine-merchants who had managed to save some pre-war wines and was a real friend, but good wines in large quantities were not there.

That was twenty-five years ago, and today, having reached the age of reason, I cannot help thinking that I must have been mad at the time. How could any meal possibly be a success under such conditions? Yet it was a great success.

If you hesitate to believe me, and I grant you that you have good cause to do so, go to the place where the British Museum keeps old newspapers and look up those published on 17 October 1944 and you will find a report of what the Minister of Food said at the Luncheon of the Wine and Food Society, on 16 October. I remember the date because it was the eve of our wedding anniversary, 17 October 1900. You will not find anything about the Menu itself, happily, but I shall never forget it; the worst meal we ever had! The first course was scallops, fair enough, the main dish was Partridge Bonne Femme, and the last an apple and sultana pudding. Of course, everybody knew that Partridge was the stage name of some bird that never was a partridge, but anybody's guess. They had wings and legs but no feet, which made Barry Neame say that they were seagulls, but I am sure that he was wrong. What little flesh was on the breast was not in the least fishy and the Chef had made the Bonne Femme of vegetables as rich as the bird was poor. What made the occasion a success was Kay Thomas and the Minister of Food. Kay Thomas was at the time the private secretary of Ben MacPeake, the head of *Good Housekeeping*, but became a Director soon after. She had not only made the table plan and had attended to all details before the meal but she flitted about during the lunch with what must have been just the right few words to members of the Press and others, making everybody feel that we had won the war and that the Algerian was not too bad after all!

It was my old friend Jack Drummond, who was there with Anne Wilbraham, once one of his students and then his wife, who had not only got the Minister of Food, but had given him the right idea about the aims and objects of the Society. A. J. A. Symons, who spoke ever so much better than I could, would not have spoken better than, if as well as, the Minister of Food did that day. It was the most unexpected and

the most wonderful gift imaginable! Little did I ever think
that both the Drummonds and their little daughter would
one day be murdered by a mad Italian farmer in France.

After that meal Barry Neame of the Hind's Head at Bray
came to me and said he would give a lunch on two different
days that would be a surprise and a joy to any pernickety
gastronome. The price would be the same as the so poor meal
at the Connaught Rooms, thirty shillings, five shillings for
three courses and no bread for the food, and twenty-five shillings for wines and service. Barry Neame specified that there
must not be more than fifty guests at each meal and that all
would be Members of the Society; no guests and no Press.
There was still a war on at the time, but if I could get today
as fine a meal as Barry Neame gave at Bray to 100 of our
Members in two batches of fifty, I would be happy to pay
any price for it. We started with an excellent piping hot
soup of fresh vegetables and ended with treacle tart, but the
main dish was pheasants that were exactly right, tender,
moist, tasty, hung just long enough, not high, quite perfect, and as much as you cared to ask for. Not bad value
for the legal five shillings. What was much more remarkable, a greater surprise and a greater delight after four years
of acute wine shortage, was to be given a 1929 Bâtard
Montrachet, grown, bottled and shipped by my old friend
Louis Poirier, the brother of Marius Poirier, whom I had
known even longer. With the pheasant, Barry gave a
Château Lascombes 1929 which was absolutely delightful;
at the top of its form and really Claret at its best. Barry had
two Impériales of this Château and he gave one of these
priceless giants at each of the two luncheons. An Impériale
is the largest bottle in which the best Claret is bottled and
it will serve fifty but no more, which is why Barry had
limited to fifty the Members he would have on each occasion. What a gift! It would have been a great treat at any
time before the war, but after more than four years of
austerity it was absolutely wonderful.

I

Needless to say, there was nowhere in or near London where we could hope to get a meal in a class comparable to what we had at the Hind's Head, and I dare not ask our Members to come to a poor three-course five-shilling meal again; the success of the so-called Victory Luncheon at the Connaught Rooms in October 1944 had been a near-miracle, never to happen again.

The Society had no more Meetings—Luncheons, Dinners, and Tastings we called Meetings—until World War II ended on 5 May 1945, with the unconditional surrender of Germany, long before fighting stopped in the Far East.

During most of the post-war years at 30 Grosvenor Gardens, I had the good fortune to have Marjorie Fletcher as Secretary. She was, indeed, a treasure. Intelligent and dependable, she could and did deal with correspondence just as well as I would have done, if not better than I would have done, when I happened to fly to and back from the U.S.A. on short visits. Her devotion to what was called duty in those days would be quite beyond belief today. Her memory was exceptional. I remember overhearing her telling one of the Members, as we were leaving a City Company where we had had dinner: 'Do you not remember that we dined in this Hall last year, and you sat at the top table and Mr. so-and-so sat at the foot; tonight he was at the top and you were at the foot.' Fair enough!

XV. THE STAGE

As a child, I never saw a pantomime any more than a game of cricket; pantomimes and cricket are two English institutions which have never crossed the English Channel. During the Christmas and New Year holidays we had the Cirque d'Hiver, a first-class circus the floor of which could and did become a lake; we also had the Châtelet where they gave fantastic shows; I have never forgotten the last scene but one of *Le tour du monde en 80 jours*. As the two travellers were in sight of land, on the last day, and night-fall, their boat capsized in a rough sea and they had to swim. I have never seen a rough sea on any stage since.

The first real play which I remember as a teenager is *La Dame aux Camélias* at the Théâtre Sarah Bernhardt, with the great Sarah in the title role. It must have been in 1892 or 1893, *en matinée*. My mother's father, *grandpère* Dardoize, who had been an ardent admirer of Sarah in his younger days, took me to see her and warned me that she was no longer what she was *avant la guerre*—that was the war of 1870—when she was lovely! I thought that she was still lovely, but I never dreamt that the day would come, as it did, when I would take my daughter Jeanne, nearly thirty years later in 1920, to see Sarah Bernhardt in Daniel, her last play, and that I would tell Jeanne almost word for word what *grandpère* Dardoize had told me. But poor Sarah at eighty was no longer lovely!

Before 1914, the London Wine Trade Club had its own Dramatic Society, which gave a performance once a year for the benefit of the Wine and Spirit Benevolent Society. All the male members of any play were members of the Club, and there were only two that were at all good—by amateur standards of course. They were Charles Cary Elwes of Parkington's, and Harry E. King of Bashfords. For female members of the cast, the practice was to look around, and trust to luck.

On 12 February 1912, the Wine Trade Club Dramatic Society gave two plays at the Royal Court Theatre, Sloane Square, the second of which was a real play *The Man from Blankley* whilst the first was a short piece of nonsense called *My French Friend*. I had written it and the Lord Chamberlain had allowed in writing that it might be acted in public. As it happened, it made everybody laugh but me. The plot, if plot it may be called, was for a Frenchman (Harry King) to give an elderly widow (Mrs. Ford) more Champagne than she ever had before, and get her, not drunk, but 'tiddly'. Had we been professionals we would have drunk the Champagne before the play started and filled the empty Magnum with lemonade. But we were novices, amateurs, and we had on the stage a real and full Magnum with a real beast of a cork! When Sutton Bendle, of Harveys of Bristol, whose part was that of the Frenchman's friend who had volunteered to act as *sommelier*, tried to get the cork out of the Magnum of Champagne, the top of the cork broke and the rest remained tightly wedged in the neck so that not a drop of wine could come out. He had no corkscrew and there were none in sight, so that all he could do was to pretend to fill the glasses at the table; all that the guests could do was to pretend that they were drinking wine from empty glasses, and the poor widow had to pretend that she was tiddly when she really was most painfully dry! As the house was packed with Wine Trade people who knew all about broken corks, they laughed and laughed, and cheered, but I didn't, and I never attempted to write another play.

The only actor that I ever knew at all well was Gerald du Maurier, who was also the only actor to be a member of the Saintsbury Club. His generosity was beyond praise, almost beyond belief. I once asked him, when I was President of the French Benevolent Society, for the loan of his theatre for a Charity Matinée by a French troupe in London at the time. He not only let us have the theatre without any payment whatsoever for electricity, stage hands, and other necessary expenses, but he had volunteers to take charge of the cloakroom so that we should have all cloakroom tips taken! I remember him telling me that he had once arranged for his wife to give a supper and look after Yvonne Printemps whilst he would entertain at the Garrick Club with Sacha Guitry, her husband, after their show. But Yvonne had somehow managed to slip away and got a taxi to the Garrick Club. She rushed up the stairs but was quickly followed and overtaken by the night porter who told her that she must have been making a mistake as no ladies were admitted. 'I know,' Yvonne told him, 'but I am no lady!' Sacha, du Maurier and the rest of the party had just arrived, so she went in with them to the private rooms, in those days on the right of the steps.

They had at the Garrick Club in the early twenties a very old day porter, a small, white-haired man known as Monkey Brand. I arrived one day at lunchtime, at the same time as the famous actor Oscar Asche, who, of course, was a member and went up the steps whilst I was a visitor, and waited to ask Monkey Brand for my host, Gerald Duckworth, Chairman at the time of the Garrick Club Wine Committee. Monkey Brand had left his box and was up the stairs asking Oscar Asche for his name. He was, naturally enough, annoyed, to put it mildly, not to be known anywhere, but to be asked for his name at the Garrick Club was the limit, and I shall never forget the way he glared from his six foot something height, at poor little Monkey Brand on the steps below him and spat out his name: Oscar Asche. I never saw Monkey Brand again when I went to the Garrick Club!

On what is called the legitimate stage, actors and actresses must have trained memories which they can trust; they

have to be word perfect. They cannot take liberties with
their text as music hall artistes are allowed and expected to
do. My memory is now patchy because of old age, but it
used to be fairly good years ago. Now it is very short-lived.
I have never read an after-dinner speech on special occasions when more than a few words were demanded; I
always wrote it first and learned it by heart. The last time it
happened was on 28 February 1967, at the Dorchester, my
ninetieth birthday. I spoke for twenty minutes without a
note, haste, nor hesitation. I had written it all down myself
the day before, read and re-read it that day, and I knew it
by heart that evening. But I could not have done it the next
evening, and I had forgotten what I had been talking about
on that evening a few weeks afterwards.

The late Lord Norwich, whom I long knew as Duff
Cooper, had a much better memory. On 21 April 1932, at
the Saintsbury Club Dinner, at Vintners' Hall, Duff Cooper
was sitting on my right and Hilaire Belloc was in the Chair;
somebody (whose name I now forget) called upon the Chairman for his recently published *Heroic Poem in praise of
Wine*; Belloc flatly refused, adding that he did not remember more than two lines of it. 'I know it all,' whispered
Duff Cooper to me, and I asked him whether he could and
would recite it there and then. He said that he would, and
he did. Of course, it was to him that Hilaire Belloc had
dedicated his great poem, and he had evidently read and
re-read it, but it is a very long piece indeed. When he came
to that great line:

　　　Dead lucre; burnt ambition; Wine is best
he paused and hesitated: there was no applause, not a sound;
we were all spellbound. Belloc gave him the next line, and
Duff went on to the end without another hitch. Of course,
when he sat down he got an ovation which he richly
deserved, but knowing as I did that he never had a line of
the poem in front of him or up his sleeve, I was amazed at
his memory.

What I cannot understand is how anybody can memorize notes as if they were words. I shall never forget a most remarkable music memory—a real *tour de force*.

The occasion was the annual Guests' Dinner of the Savage Club years ago, when I was a Savage and the Savage Club was at Adelphi Terrace. The dinner was at the Victoria Hotel, Northumberland Avenue, and the pianist Mark Hambourg, who was a Savage, had promised to give us a surprise, and he did. There were three grand pianos on the platform, in one line. After dinner, of course, Mark sat down at the first, on the left, where all he could see was the back of the head of his daughter, who sat at the next piano; all she could see was the back of the head of her sister who sat at the third piano. The father and his two daughters played six hands superbly for a long but all too short time—a miracle of both memory and timing.

XVI. VINTAGE CHARTS

THE Winter Number 1934 of *Wine and Food* carried an article on the 1934 and 1933 vintages which I had taken great pains to write with the best possible second-hand but reliable information from friends in all the chief European vineyards. Later I did the same for the 1935 and 1936 vintages, but I had soon realized that those Vintage Reports failed in their mission, or rather fell between two stools: they did not teach much if anything to those of our Members who were in the Wine Trade, and there were many in the early years of the Society's existence; and as to the others, the doctors, lawyers, men and women of the world who had all manner of other and greater interests, they could not be expected to memorize what they had read about the merits and demerits of various vintages in the Winter Numbers of *Wine and Food* one year or two and three years before. Yet I felt sure that many of our readers, and their friends as well, were by no means indifferent to the question of good and bad vintages. This is why I came to the conclusion that it might be a good thing to prepare and publish, in a handy vest-pocket size, a kind of ready-reckoner card giving an immediate answer to anybody asking: 'Was such or such a year a good or a bad vintage for Port, Claret, Burgundy, Hock or Champagne?' I started with an attempt at assessing the merits of seven of the more popular wines during the immediate past seven years, but the little squat square card did not 'look' right, so I tried fourteen years and then twenty-one, which both A. J. and I agreed was both a better looking card and a much more useful one, since there were many of our Members who either still had in their cellars twenty-year-old wines, or, if not, could still buy some of them.

Our Vintage Charts were from the first a great success, a success due equally to A.J.'s share in their production as to me in their conception. I certainly did my best to give to each wine its due marking year by year, without fear or favour, and it was no easy task; but A.J. wrote in his fine gothic hand the figures of the chart, and he also discovered the firm—and there was then one firm only that was capable of doing it really well—who printed our Charts on celluloid. I am quite sure that the same figures printed in exactly the same way but on paper or cardboard, although they would have been very much cheaper, would never have had the same appeal, nor would they have had any-thing like the same lasting quality. Before the war we could sell them at 6d. each or five shillings a dozen, but after the war their price was a shilling each or ten shillings per dozen.

The success of our first little Wine Chart was so gratifying that we thought we might publish every year a revised edition of the same Chart, adding the latest vintage at the bottom of the card and taking off the topmost vintage, as well as giving different wines and years a higher or lower marking according to any experience gained during the past twelve months. We also decided to publish other Charts, the first being devoted to Port, giving an assessment of the merits of Port Vintages for over a hundred years, from 1834 to date; the second was confined to the latest twenty vintages of the wines of Germany, with separate markings for the wines of the Rhinegau, Rhinehesse, Nahe, Pala-tinate, Moselle, Saar and Ruwer. The demand for both these 'specialized' Charts, however, was not very great, whereas the 'General Chart', the original one, has never ceased to be by far our most popular 'publication'. We must have sold over a quarter of a million copies, but the mone-tary gain resulting from its sale has been more than offset, in my opinion, by the loss of the friends we once had among wine-merchants.

Nobody can be more fully aware than I am that it is quite impossible to give a final and reliable assessment of the merits and demerits of the more popular wines made every year. My idea, when I first devised the Wine Chart and graded the wines of twenty-one vintages from 0 'No good' to 7 'The best', was in the first place to give some kind of guidance to vintages which were known to have been really good or absolutely bad—like 1929 and 1930, for instance; and in the second place to give wine-minded people a start for an argument: it is only when we do not care and do not mind that we do not argue. Hardly two persons, even the more knowledgeable persons, can be expected to agree regarding the merits and demerits of every vintage, and arguments, discussions and comparisons of wine interest were responsible for the sale of our little celluloid Vintage Charts. Although I have always taken the greatest possible care in deciding upon the figures shown, I know that these figures can always be challenged, and that as good judges of wine as I am, and some better judges than I am, have every right to disagree with my verdict. I have never minded that. On the contrary, I welcome criticisms and arguments as the best proof of interest in a subject that has been so dear to me for so long.

The number of 'points' given to different wines of various vintages on our Vintage Charts may be considered right by some and wrong by others, but all are in fairness bound to agree that the Society has never sold and has never intended to sell any wine to its Members, so that its assessments, appraisals or judgements are entirely disinterested.

XVII. THE FRENCH BENEVOLENT
SOCIETY

T HE French Benevolent Society was founded in London
by Comte Alfred d'Orsay in 1842, at a time when there
were a greater number than ever before or since of French
people who were unemployed and unemployable, very poor,
mostly old or very old, the jetsam and flotsam of several
receding tides of French émigrés as far back as the French
Revolution, fifty years earlier, Napoleon's dictatorship and
the comeback of the Bourbons. From 1909 to 1919 the
President of the Society was J. L. P. Lebègue, a Bordeaux-
born wine shipper who had built up, in London, a very
successful firm dealing exclusively with French wines.
Louis de Ayala, whose only daughter, Marie, is the wife of
Nubar Gulbenkian, Emile Guillet, whose youngest son is
the husband of my daughter Jeanne, and myself were members of the committee of the French Benevolent Society,
before 1914, by the wish or by the request of Monsieur
Lebègue, who did not ask or expect us to attend any of the
committee meetings; the President preferred to deal with
the affairs of the Society single-handed.

Incidentally, if the name of Lebègue became famous, as
it did, among all wine-conscious people in England, it had
nothing to do with the original J. L. P. Lebègue: it was
entirely due to the vision and energy of Guy Prince after
World War II, when he was the head of the Lebègue firm
and gave those famous Lebègue wine-tastings under the
London Bridge Railway Arches. One day, in 1919, when I
was back at my 24 Mark Lane office, a clerk from the
Lebègue firm came to ask me to come with him to see
Monsieur Lebègue who had sent him and wished to see me.
His office was in Mincing Lane, a stone's throw from Mark

Lane, and I went. Although he was old enough to be my father, J. L. P. Lebègue was erect, quick, and as alert as a very much younger man, so that I was quite surprised, almost shocked, when his first words to me as I came into his private room were 'When I die'. He insisted with such force that I had in the end to promise him that at his death, whenever that might be, I would put my name down as a candidate and, if elected President, that I would do my best, as he had done himself, for the French Benevolent Society. Little did he or I know on that day that he was to die two or three weeks later, and that I would be elected President in his place right away. I was far from happy about it, as I had so much else to do, after the much too long break of the war, but an incident which happened shortly after my election made me feel that the Society was well worth any time and attention I could spare. A French woman living in Paris had lost her husband, killed in 1914, and her only son, killed in 1918. She had a daughter, eighteen or nineteen years old, who was so depressed that the doctor had advised her mother to send her for a month or so to a convent, in England, as a thorough change of scene, company, food and so on to help take her mind away from her grief. But it did not work. On the contrary, the poor girl became delirious and the Mother Superior of the convent was obliged to send for a doctor, who was obliged to certify the girl as insane. The Mother Superior wrote to the girl's mother who wired immediately asking for her daughter to be sent back to her, but the Matron of the place where the girl had been sent said that she could not let her go without an order from the Home Office. The Mother Superior was told that she had better try the French Benevolent Society. This is how she came to me. By sheer luck it happened that the Home Secretary at the time was Edward Short, brother-in-law of Andrew Scott, our Valparaiso Agent, and I had met him. I rang him up, hoping he would remember me, and he did. I asked him if he could see me for five minutes and he told me to come right away. I did. I got the necessary permit immediately, wired to the girl's mother to be at Boulogne the next day and meet the Folkestone boat. The next day I saw the girl and a nurse safely into a reserved compartment of the Folkestone boat train. Her mother came on board at Boulogne and went home to Paris with her daughter, who became quite normal again some time after, as her grateful mother wrote to me.

The first thing I hurried to do as President of the French Benevolent Society was to give a dinner at which an appeal would be made for the Society, and the hurry was that I was anxious for the dinner to be presided over by the French Ambassador, the venerable Paul Cambon who was, I knew, retiring and going back to France shortly after. No ticket was sold for the dinner in the great hall of the Connaught Rooms. All came by invitation, but they all knew that next to their place card there would be another card with a small pencil attached to it, on which they were expected to write their name and the amount they promised to give to the Society. Those cards were collected after the dinner and the speeches, and that night, after paying for the dinner, there was a total of just over £2,000— a great deal of money at the time, worth about £10,000 of today's money. It never happened again. My old friend William Burgess, of J. L. Denman, gave £100 and so did three other of my Wine Trade friends, whose names I am ashamed to say I cannot now remember. But I do remember Ian Campbell telling me some time later that he and his partner Neville Reid had agreed, before going to the dinner, knowing that there would be an after-dinner collection, to give the same sum, £5 5s. od. The next morning, however, when they met at their 25 Mark Lane office, both were somewhat embarrassed or unhappy until each had confessed to the other that they had given £10 10s. od. instead of £5 5s. od. Both Scots! Rightly or wrongly, I believe that it was a kind of generous welcome back from members of the

Wine Trade who had not seen me for five years. I knew, however, that there was a Wine Trade Benevolent Society which all those in the Wine Trade were in duty bound to support, and that some of my friends also had some pet charity of their own, besides which I had sufficient common-sense to realize that the people best qualified to support a French charity were the French people who lived in England—and there were still a great number of pre-1914 French residents in London during the twenties; so we switched over from a dinner a year by invitation, to an annual *Bal et Souper* by ticket, the number of which had to be limited at a time when *la valse* and *le quadrille* required far more floor space than the modern hugging together on an over-crowded floor. The French Benevolent Society's annual Ball, usually at the Hyde Park Hotel, became one of the Season's social functions, always attended by the French Ambassador, his wife and daughter or daughters, as well as some of the Embassy personnel. French banks in London such as the Credit Lyonnais and Société Générale sold tickets to some of their wealthy customers, who had financial, commercial or industrial interests in France, and there were some francophile members of the English aristocracy, such as Lord Bessborough and Lord Burnham, who came, besides, of course, all the well-to-do members of the French colony in London. The last of the Society's balls at the Hyde Park Hotel was in 1933, as the economic temperature had dropped to near freezing point. Fortunately, the needs of the Society were by then not nearly so great as they had been. By 1939, the number of French people in London was but a fifth of what it was in 1914 and there were not many left of the really old ones. The Society managed to stage a Charity Sale at Claridges, in 1942, to celebrate its centenary, but war conditions were not propitious. However, General de Gaulle and Madame de Gaulle attended and were very gracious. After the war came the Welfare State, pensions for the old, National Health benefits for all—

French or not made no difference, since they had paid as they earned, like the rest, which is how the French Benevolent Society lost most of its clients, and why its President resigned.

The French people in England during the twenties, who needed and were given the assistance of the French Benevolent Society, belong to two different categories—the residents and the visitors. Before World War I anybody on the Continent in trouble with the police of their native land, very often for differences of opinion on political matters, could come to England without any passport, identity card or permit of any kind. As all such refugees were well aware that if they did not behave themselves they would be sent back not only to their native land, but to the police authorities, they always did behave very well. In 1871, when the disastrous 1870–71 war was coming to an end, there was a short-lived but violent rising of Communists in Paris, who burned down the Hôtel de Ville, or town hall. A number of them, including Rochefort, their leader, escaped to England, most of them with a wife and children, knowing, as they did, that France would not be safe for them for quite a long time. Some of their children went back to France, and some grew up, worked, married in England and, in old age, chose to stay in England with their children and grandchildren, rather than go back to France where they had few or no contacts with their parents' relations. Even if they had not married, they had, in England, after fifty or sixty, or even more years, many friends and none in France. I remember a dear little old lady who came to the Society every Thursday, not only to be given her week's pension, but to have a chat about old days in Soho. She had earned her living with her needle; she had been very well paid—but not of course by modern standards—by some of the leading fashion houses. Then old age and illness came before the Welfare State, her savings went and her mind became unbalanced. She was picked up by the police unconscious in the street and taken to hospital where they found that she was dying of malnutrition. She had not had any food whatsoever for some days. Why? Because she had no money—she had put the money we had given her on Thursday, for safety, into a red pillar box, which she believed at the time to be the Post Office Savings Bank. The poor old dear was normal and reasonable enough nearly always, and if a lapse of memory were to qualify anybody for a mental home, new mental homes would have to be built by the hundred! Her right place was the French home at de Courcel Road, Brighton, where a number of French men and women, when old and poor, are well looked after. However, she did not want to be well looked after. I am quite sure that she had been the most law-abiding person, all her life, but there was in her blood some ancestral craving for freedom which made the most hospitable home, with meals served on time and a bolted front door, no better than a de luxe prison. She would rather go hungry and be free. She was unwise and unfortunate, but not mad—maybe a border-line case.

As a matter of fact, half or more of our old 'clients' could not help being old, but would not have been, as most of them were, utterly destitute had it not been for a screw loose or missing. There were border-line cases among the 'visitors' category of our Society's clients but they were few. There were visitors of all ages, young and old, but mostly young, however, and all had to get a passport to land and a permit from the Labour Exchange if they wished to work. I ought to have said most of them, rather than all, as I can remember a regular visitor who came year after year and asked us to give him a free passage back to France. A number of other visitors asked us the same thing once, and no more; most of them were very young and had lost their head, their heart or their money in England, and did not know how to get home. They had no money but they all had a passport. Our regular had no passport but he had *une casquette*, a leather cap, the type of

cap which railway porters wear in France. He was an old
sailor, but not an old man; a border case, but not mad. Some
time in the early summer, some kind of wanderlust came
upon Jean (I forget what his name was, but Jean will do).
He waited for the Paris train to arrive at Boulogne, probably at some distance not to attract attention, and when the
platform was black with passengers from the train, he came
forward, wearing his *casquette*, took up somebody's box or
boxes, got on board, pocketed his tip, and disappeared
below, where he managed to find a dark corner to hide.
When the boat reached Folkestone, he remained in the
lavatory or some other hiding place and waited for his chance
to get ashore unobserved; so started his annual walking
tour of England. He never had any trouble with the police
or anybody, but he managed to get food enough on the
'bob a job' or 'bun a job' basis, until he had had enough,
and wanted to get back to France. His *casquette* was of no
use to him at Folkestone or Dover; he could not get on
board, and had to come to the French Benevolent Society
for a free passage home. We had his passport in our safe—
I had taken it from him the first time he had come to us,
when I had told him sternly not to do it again. But it had
made no difference! I had not the heart to take his *casquette*
from him.

In fairness to the French Consulate in London, I should
record the fact that the French Benevolent Society was
dealing then with repatriations for the Consulate, paying
for the return to France of stranded French people in
England, but each year an account was sent by the Society
to the Consulate, and eventually the Society was paid back
in full.

K

XVIII. TV CHEFS

MARCEL BOULESTIN was the first TV Chef, and nobody was more surprised than he was himself to occupy this exalted position. He was a very charming little man with a remarkable gift for making friends, but not for making money or keeping it when he made any. Very intelligent, highly sensitive, he had an eye for beauty and an ear for music, a born artist with a keen and sound critical sense. He loved writing and he wrote very well, with an engaging directness and simplicity, in French first of all, of course, and, later, in English. He was quite young when he first came to live in London to learn the language, and he quickly learnt it: he also learnt to like the English and came to love England as his adopted country. So, after World War I, in which he served as an interpreter with the B.E.F., he came back to London and made it his home. He had no job, and when asked what he did for a living, he would say: '*Je bricole.*' There is no English word for *bricoler*; it means doing all sorts of odd things which happen to be to one's liking at the time, such as attending first nights and being the London musical and literary critic for *Comoedia* and other Paris journals; decorating and choosing the furniture for the homes of his friends and of their friends; translating English books into French; selling French pictures and drawings in London on behalf of French artists, and so on. It was when he had been to see Heinemann, the publishers, to offer them some sketches by his friend Laboureur, which they bought to illustrate some of their books, that he asked more in jest than earnest: 'I suppose that you wouldn't like me to write a cookery book for you?' Much to his surprise and delight, the answer was:

'Indeed, it is just the sort of book that we would like.' And they gave him there and then a contract and an advance royalty of £10. It was the first rung of the ladder which led Marcel to become a restaurateur of world-wide renown and the first TV Chef.

At that time, Boulestin had never thought about cooking, let alone done any cooking, but he had always enjoyed good food and good wine as a young man in his native Périgord, the land of truffles, and ever since, as the always welcome guest of the many friends he had made in Paris and in London. He had great taste and he had the gift of expression, which is why his first cookery book was such an immediate success, soon to be followed by others and by articles on cookery in the National Press, which were more immediately rewarding than royalties. Having become almost overnight the most popular cookery book writer in London, Boulestin was urged to start a restaurant, which he did, with the financial aid of friends and well-wishers who had great faith in him. His first restaurant was at the corner of Leicester Square and Panton Street, a modest venture, soon to be followed by a more ambitious one in Southampton Street, by Covent Garden, which is still flourishing. As TV Chef, Boulestin was a great success: his simple bonhomie, his lack of ostentation, and the engaging friendliness of his delivery appealed to a rapidly growing number of viewers. Then came the war, and the tragedy of Boulestin's death in a military hospital.

After the war, the B.B.C. came to me and asked me, knowing as they did that Boulestin had been a friend of mine, if I could recommend to them another one of my French friends in London to take his place. I told them that I did not know any, but that I thought that an English friend of mine might well be a suitable person: he was as different from Boulestin as anybody could be, and he was no professional cook, but the son and the brother of two gifted actresses; he was a born showman with a funny face that should be an asset on the screen: his name was Philip Harben: he got the job and, as all know, he was a great success.

XIX. NO PLANNING—JUST LUCK

THERE was no more colourful figure in 'Reims by night' than Ernest Dowling during the last two decades of the nineteenth century and the first decade of the twentieth, the thirty years of the great Champagne boom. Red faced and with red hair and whiskers, rotund and benevolent, he was entrusted by the Pommery Champagne firm with the delicate mission of seeing that male visitors had not only as much Pommery Champagne to drink as was good for them, but had what was known as a really good time—which was not nearly so good for them. Why such a mission had been given to an Irishman, nobody could tell, but nobody ever denied that he was the man for the job. Few people in Reims, however, knew that Ernest Dowling had problems of his own: he looked after his old mother, at home, and he had got his young brother a job in the Pommery cellars. There did not appear to be any hope for this young Dowling to get a responsible position in the cellars, but his chance came when, in the nineties, Prince Galitzine, who owned large vineyards in the Crimea, had an idea that he might as well have his own Champagne: he wrote to Messrs. Pommery of Reims and asked them whether they could recommend a man who would be willing to come to the Crimea, settle there and make his Crimean wine sparkle. Whether no French member of the staff would go, or whether Messrs. Pommery did not wish to part with any French member of their staff, I cannot say, but young Dowling did go and was quite a success. When the Bolshevik Revolution reached the Crimea, Prince Galitzine and all his people left, but Dowling remained, with his wife and daughter. The Bolsheviks looted the princely cellars, of course, but did not harm Dowling: on the contrary, they gave him their blessing and told him to make as much and as good wine as possible. Later the counter-revolution troops of General Wrangel also came to the Crimea, congratulated Dowling upon his loyalty and told him to 'carry on'. All seemed serene enough, but after the Reds and the Whites came the Blues: a party of Bluejackets came along with orders to evacuate all British subjects. Dowling was furious. He argued that he was no British subject at all but an Irishman, and that he did not want to be evacuated, but orders are orders: he and his wife and his daughter were bundled on board a destroyer and landed at Constantinople, with three boxes of personal effects; as a matter of fact, their personal effects were in two boxes, and Crimean wine in the third. After protests, which nobody heeded, and a very unhappy stay, they were all three the guests of the Navy once more and shipped to Alexandria, where they spent another unhappy time, but eventually they were dumped with a number of other British evacuees at Tilbury in 1919. By that time I had been demobilized and I had at long last returned to Mark Lane. It was, indeed, lucky for Dowling. He rang me up from Tilbury, on landing, told me how it was that he was there, with no money, no job, no hope, and asked me to come to his help. He must have been amazed when I just asked him whether he would be willing to go to Australia right away. Of course, he was ready to go anywhere. His luck was in, definitely. He was just in time, and he sailed for Australia, from Tilbury, two days later.

It so happened that I had received a letter that very day from Sir Josiah Symon of Adelaide, asking me to try and get one of Pommery's cellar experts to come to Australia and show his people how to make sparkling wine. I sent him Dowling, his wife and his daughter, with two boxes of their personal effects: Dowling gave me the third box with the Galitzine wine.

XX. A DICTIONARY OF GASTRONOMY

FROM 1904, when A. S. Gardiner asked me to write about Champagne for the *Wine Trade Review*, and 1933, when Michael Sadleir asked me to write three of the books of Constable's Wine Library and to edit the others, I had been writing practically non-stop about wine, with the break, of course, of World War I. When A. J. A. Symons and I started the Wine and Food Society, in October 1933, I soon realized that our Members would expect to be given some information about food as well as wine, and I was painfully aware of the fact that I knew nothing about it. I had probably enjoyed more than my fair share of fine food in various parts of the world during my 'Champagne' years, but that could not be of the slightest interest to anybody but me. What our Members were likely to ask for were the names, the origin, the varieties, qualities, and so on of every kind of edible meat, fish, vegetable or fruit. Having been told how to know what was best to choose and buy, they would also expect to be told which were the best ways of dealing with it in the kitchen. Could it be done? Of course, it could be done and it was done. How? Hard work during ten years, off and on, when the chance came.

As a modest token of the Society's intentions to deal with food, some day, our first publication was a little paperback about cheese. I gathered from helpful and most willing cheesemongers the names of most home made and imported cheeses, as well as bits and pieces of information, and then set it all up in the way of questions and answers, which is why the booklet was given the title of *A Catechism about Cheese*. But this was mere play; not real work. The real work was partly, if not mostly, done at the Kensington Natural History Museum. I told the Librarian there, a very kind and knowledgeable man, that my ambition was to write a Dictionary of Gastronomy. He knew which were the books in which I was most likely to find the kind of information I was looking for. His help was invaluable. What I found to be a handicap at the time was to be without an office. No. 6 Little Russell Street was the registered address of the Wine and Food Society, but not its office: it was the office of the First Edition Club. In the main hall, where the first editions of the year were exhibited, there was but one table, with a telephone on it and a chair before it. It was from that table that A. J. A. Symons dealt with the correspondence and the affairs of both the First Edition Club and the Wine and Food Society, with the help of a secretary and typist out of sight, near the entrance. If I had a cheque or a letter to sign, A.J. would rise, graciously give me his chair, and stand by until I rose and went out. We usually discussed the Society's affairs at lunch time.

I had the good fortune in 1935 to meet Gordon Boggon when he and his wife, my wife and myself were the guests of George Messenger and his wife. Gordon and I became good friends. He was the Managing Director of Mather and Crowther, an important advertising concern responsible at the time for the successful 'Eat more fruit' campaign. I have an idea that Gordon may have had in mind that I might be of use if some attempt were made to start a 'Drink more wine' campaign. Anyhow, I was offered, and gladly accepted to join Mather and Crowther as a consultant. The fee was small but acceptable and unimportant; what was far more important and a real joy to me was the fact that I was given an office, all to myself at the top of the building, overlooking the Savoy Chapel garden, away from all street and other noises. It was in the peace of that office that I gave up all hope of ever publishing a Dictionary of Gastronomy. I had too much else to do: the functions of the Society and the publication of the quarterly had to be given priority. There was no sense in starting with the letter A when it appeared quite possible, not to say likely, that it must be many years before I reached the letter Z.

I decided instead to deal with each of our chief types of food. The book on Fish, for instance, would tell all you wanted to know about fish, and nothing else and however long you might have to wait for books on meat, or fruit, or anything else made no difference to the fact that you were the lucky owner of the best reference book on Fish!

As it happened, the nine Sections of subjects which I called *A Concise Encyclopaedia of Gastronomy* were published, one each year, much more regularly than I had feared would be the case. This was due on the one hand to the war, which put an end to the Society's functions and gave me more time and, on the other hand, to the fact that Oliver Simon and The Curwen Press were wonderfully good to me; they managed to find the necessary paper somehow when nobody else could.

Section I of the *Concise Encyclopaedia of Gastronomy*, 'Sauces', was published in 1939 from No. 6 Little Russell Street, in the autumn, when I had to take the chair and the duties of my poor friend A. J. A. Symons who was at his mother's house or in hospital, suffering from the somewhat mysterious illness which killed him. Section II, 'Fish', was published in 1940, also from Little Russell Street, but Number III, 'Vegetables', was published from Little Hedgecourt, the only address of the Wine and Food Society, and my own. The next six Numbers, i.e. IV, 'Cereals'; V, 'Fruit'; VI, 'Birds and their Eggs'; VII, 'Meat'; VIII, 'Wine'; and IX, 'Cheese'; were all published from No. 30 Grosvenor Gardens, the Society's office from 1942 to 1961.

All the nine Sections were mostly published as paperbacks, but there were nevertheless a fair number bound, and well bound, by Pippa Woodman. Bound copies were naturally more costly, but it made no difference to the sales.

Whenever Curwen managed to get some more paper of the right quality, they reprinted one or the other of the nine Sections which was sold forthwith. Of course, the fact that I had the National Magazine Company distributing my books to the book trade helped me greatly. Between 1939 and 1946, the number of copies of the *Concise Encyclopaedia of Gastronomy* added up to fifteen thousand copies, quite a lot of books as well as a fair amount of money.

Had I been a sensible person, I would have been satisfied and given all my attention to the Wine and Food Society which had been out of action, all but its Magazine, during the war years. But I was not a sensible person. I might have been called a perfectionist or a silly ass; it was all the same! It worried me to think that a thing like Sugar, of such capital importance in Gastronomy, had to be left out of the Encyclopaedia because it was neither fish nor fruit nor with a place in any of the other Sections. Here is my chance, I thought, to publish the *Dictionary of Gastronomy*: all the entries in the nine Sections of the Encyclopaedia could be taken out and set in their alphabetical order, with Sugar, Tea, Coffee and other missing entries given their right place. In order not to compete with the Encyclopaedia, the Dictionary would not have more than the shortest possible commentary for each entry, and no recipes whatsoever. Unfortunately Curwen could not print it: there was a long queue of orders awaiting their turn and they had been so good to me during the war years that I had no right to pester them. Much more unfortunately, I was given the name and address of some Manchester printers who had paper and would do the job. There was no hurry. I could easily have waited a year, or two or ten years until Curwen would do it. But I did not wait and I sent my text to Manchester. Trying to be as fair as I can, I must say that they produced a slim book which looked well enough printed and bound. On closer examination, however, you found that a PATE was meant to be pâté, and the one same page had been printed twice and bound in two different parts of the book. I was furious. I had sold the book, before it was printed, to Farrar, Straus, of New York, who were sent the number of printed sheets which they had bought; they never paid for them and were never asked to do so. I gave away a number of copies and we did sell some, but the bulk of the print was pulped, and I made up my mind to forget about it for ever! As a matter of fact, I had very good cause to be so much happier with the *Concise Encyclopaedia of Gastronomy* which was published soon after by Collins in a two guineas single volume, with all missing entries put in, and an Index which made it as easy to find what you happened to be looking for as in an A to Z Dictionary.

One Saturday, during the summer of 1967, Leonard Russell of the *Sunday Times* and his wife Dilys Powell were lunching with us at Little Hedgecourt—they have a very nice weekend house not far from us as the crow flies—and I was quite taken by surprise when Leonard Russell asked me why I did not bring my old *Dictionary of Gastronomy* up to date and publish a revised edition. I told him that I hated the book and why. He said that he loved the book, and why. During the past many years—maybe twenty— since I had given it to him, it had been one of his bedside books, and that whenever in doubt about the meaning of a word about food or drink, in English or in French, he had always found the right answer in my book. Accents did not worry him, and anyhow it would not take me long to put the missing ones in their proper place. I even believe that he said something like having the book published by the *Sunday Times* if I would not publish it myself. I told him that it might be better if he talked it over with George Rainbird (whose publishing house is now a cousin of the *Sunday Times*), which he did. I believe, from what I heard from both of them, that they quite agreed about the desirability of publishing a revised edition of my old

Dictionary, but it took some time to come to a final decision whether it had better be a smaller and cheaper book, or a more important and more expensive one. In the end, it was left to George Rainbird and his organization to decide. They decided that it had better be a big book, an important book of reference, and they asked Robin Howe to supply a range of recipes for most of the entries in the Dictionary.

This is why and how *A Dictionary of Gastronomy* by André L. Simon and Robin Howe came to be published, in London, in 1969!

XXI. BOOK COLLECTING

PRINTER'S ink was my first love. I was given books long before I was given *eau rougie* at home or *abondance* at school—two names for the same mixture of tap water and some nondescript red wine. When I left school and until we came to live in London, I had many occasions to enjoy here and there an odd glass or two of all kinds of different wines, but I do not believe that I ever bought a bottle of fine wine. What little money I had to spare I spent on books; chiefly historical books and most of them dealing with the Napoleonic era.

Soon after the Wine Trade Club was founded however in 1908, in London, I agreed to be the Chairman of the Education Committee. I promised to give a series of lectures to members of the Club, at first, but soon after to all employees in the Wine Trade (that is when the Vintners' Company opened their doors to us, and I was able to deliver my lectures in their great hall). Then it was that the necessity and urgency of having books on wine became obvious to me.

I got in touch with a number of second-hand booksellers, chiefly in England but also in France and Germany, by phone or post card, asking them to send me their catalogues to 24 Mark Lane. They did and they had no cause to regret it. I built up in five years the Wine Trade Club Library: its catalogue was published in 1913 by Grant Richards in a book of no less than 340 pages. The more modern the books the better for the lectures, but I could not resist buying for myself some old books which had no technical value whatever as far as the lectures were concerned but had for me nevertheless great charm, which is how I started in a modest way to collect books on wine. I know that the Wine Trade Club has ceased to exist but I am told that its library was given to the Guild of Masters of Wine. Being a club without premises, they have lodged the books in the Guildhall Library.

Collecting is a form of hunting; not to kill but to save the prey. The hunter or collector is bound to have many disappointments when the books he wants are nowhere to be found or cost far more than he can afford. The collector is always on the lookout for a mistake or a misprint in a book catalogue, or some wonderful bargain just round the corner. I have never forgotten, for instance, my excitement and intense joy when I saw in a second-hand book catalogue from Brighton which had been readdressed to me by my 24 Mark Lane office, a book the title of which is still clear in my mind after sixty years: *De Naturali Vinorum Historia*, Bacci. 1596. £1. I do not remember whether I wired or wrote to my wife at Brighton with the babies during my usual round of business calls in the North of England. I gave her the name and address of the bookseller and the number of the book in his catalogue. Happily she was in time. It is the first folio I bought. It is worth today over £100 but that does not matter. I cannot take it to heaven presently, but that does not matter either. I cannot see it any more (and that does matter); but it has been a friend since 1910: one of the very few friends still with me.

Bacci's *Historia* was the first real bargain of a lifetime of book collecting. It raised my hopes and made me keener than I had been before to gather a number of old books dealing with wine. Before 1914, it was not even a terribly expensive hobby.

There had been many vineyards planted and there had been much wine made during the hey-day of the Roman Empire; not only in Italy but in most parts of the Empire.

The Romans knew a great deal about different species of grapes, and viticulture, as well as wine making. Their best

writer on agriculture and viticulture, in my opinion, was
Pliny the younger or Plinius Secundus, born in A.D. 23,
whose great book was beautifully printed for the first time
in 1469; I never had the means to buy a copy nor the luck
to get any copy earlier than 1501. I had better luck with
one of Plinius's elders, Columella, born at Cadiz in 2 B.C.,
who died in Rome in A.D. 65. Although his book is a much
less important one, he gives more precise details about
species of grapes and the making of wine. Columella is,
with Cato, Varro and Palladius, one of the Latin writers
known as the geoponic authors. Their works were now and
again printed separately and I have some of them, but they
were much more usually printed together in rather fat
volumes, under the title of *Scriptores Rei Rusticae* or some
such title having the same meaning. A collection like this
was published for the first time in 1472, but I never got hold
of a copy; my two early editions of the *Scriptores* are dated
1482 and 1499. I have, however, seventeen different editions
published during the sixteenth century, including the first
edition in French, none of them except the French edition
rare and most of them temptingly cheap to buy, not to say
irresistibly so for a collector with limited means.

It was only in the later twenties when there were no
more school bills to pay, that I could afford to pay real money
for really fine books. I took a great fancy to Peter Crescens
and I spent a great deal of money getting together as many
as possible of his books. He was born in 1230 but it was not
until he was seventy years old that he decided to write a
kind of *Maison rustique* in twelve volumes; and each one
dealing with what might have been called the problems and
pleasures of life away from cities, in the heart of the country.
Which were the best grapes to grow and how to make the
best wine was one of the problems, whilst hunting and
fishing were among the pleasures. I have two manuscripts
of this remarkable old man, one written on paper, in 1414,
and the other undated but of about the same period written

on parchment, with all the capital letters, thousands of them, beautifully gilt, the gold (real gold, of course) as if put on yesterday. There is a charming coloured miniature, with blue, pink and all its colours still fresh. I am sorry to say that I have lost all record of what I paid for this treasure. I had the good fortune to get hold of the first edition of Crescens's book and I have never forgotten that I had to give 300 golden sovereigns for it, because my dearly beloved wife did not approve. Of course, it was a lot of money—but a truly beautiful book in mint state and in its original remarkable binding.

Besides the Augsburg 1471 first edition, I have three other editions of the same book printed before 1500 and about a score printed during the sixteenth century, including the two earliest editions with woodcuts and the first French edition.

Books dealing with vineyards and wine extensively if not exclusively were at first the only ones I was looking for, but it was not very long before I began to be interested in a number of books, manuscripts and documents I came across which were very attractive in themselves, but were not wine books at all; although there might be some passing mention of vineyards or wine in them. Thus when I was offered a perfect folio page of Gutenberg's Bible (1450)— the first book ever printed—my excuse for buying it was the fact that I could read on its verso Isaiah's description of how a good vineyard is to be planted. The text was slender but the temptation was great, and the £80 which I paid for a beautiful piece of early printing gave me and many of my bookish visitors, for a number of years, far greater pleasure than anything else that the same money might have bought at the time.

Of course, when you allow an exception to any of your own rules you open the door to more exceptions. How could I have helped falling in love with Platina's *De Honesta Voluptate* of 1475? Platina's real name was

Bartholomeus Sicci, and he was the librarian of the Vatican library at the time of his death. The title of his book, in English, would have been *The Art of Good Living*; full of good sense and valuable advice, but one chapter only—a good one—on wine. I bought my 1475 edition as the first edition but learnt later that it was only the first dated edition as there was an earlier undated one. I am happy to think that old Bartholomeus had the satisfaction of knowing that there was a good demand for his book as soon as it was published. I have a few editions printed before 1500 but more that were printed during the sixteenth century including the first edition in French, printed in 1505; one of the rarest.

There were two other groups of old works which I found presently in my net and made the mistake of keeping; they were books written by doctors or by churchmen. The most famous of the first was the Spanish-born Arnoldus Villanova (1238–1314), better known as Arnaud de Villeneuve; he was regarded as the most learned man of his age and kings and popes often sought his advice. Of course Arnaud de Villeneuve, like all sensible men of all times, had great faith in wine, but I am sorry to say that his little book entitled *De Vinis* has nothing whatever to do with any wine that I have ever drunk or wished to drink. It is a list of medicinal wines—all of which must have been quite horrible.

The School of Salerno eclipsed at the time the fame of the Montpellier school of medicine. There were many books published by the School, or given its blessing under the title, *Regimen Sanitatis*, a title which tempted me to buy a number of them quite unworthy of a place on my shelves. Some on the other hand were quite amusing. I have one, for instance, printed in Germany in 1513, recommending an occasional bath in warm water as part of the regime of health, with, however, a very important proviso: you must never expose your naked body to air and water without the

L

precaution of a large draught of wine, as the Queen of England always did. To prove this was no fairy tale, but a fact, there is a woodcut on the title-page of the book showing Queen Elizabeth—not the virgin queen, but her grand-mother—the queen of Henry VII, with nothing whatever on except a gold crown on her head, sitting in her wooden bath and being given a pottle of wine by her doctor.

As regards books by monks and churchmen, and books of sermons, I am bound to admit today that most of them were books which I bought solely because I loved old books, although there was in all of them something about the drinking of wine in moderation or to excess. Some of them gave some sensible comments upon the various degrees of drunkenness and sinfulness. If, for instance, we are given bad wine which makes us sick and apparently drunk, the sin is on the head of our host, not our own; we were not drunk but drugged! Fair enough. If we were given a great welcome on our return from a long and dangerous sea voyage or military campaign, a little more than just enough wine was almost inevitable and a venial sin; but if we leave our watches and wallets at home before going to a party, we obviously intend to become dead drunk. That is a real sin.

None of the founders of monastic orders, none of the Doctors of the Church, and none of the pre-Reformation preachers had a word to say against wine, one of God's gifts like our tongue and speech. There are, after all, more liars than drunkards.

The pride and rarest book of my collection, which I have kept for the last, was written by Dr. William Turner, one of the medical attendants of Queen Elizabeth, published in 1568, and given what may well be the longest title ever given to any book, beginning thus *A New Boke of the Natures and Properties of all Wines that are commonlye used in England*. It is only a little book but the first book in English to deal with wine. The fact that there is no wine in Shakespeare other than those mentioned by Turner makes me believe, rightly or wrongly, that Shakespeare must have used this little book when he had anything to say about wine; it might even have been my own copy which he owned. Who knows? Anyhow, the little book paid the penalty of being popular far too long: there are but five complete copies of it known to exist today. Of course, I knew about this so rare treasure and a number of anti-quarian booksellers also knew that if ever a copy came on the market, it must be offered to me, so I was not entirely without a chance. One afternoon, two days before Christmas, in the early twenties, Hugh Cecil Lea, who owned *The Wine and Spirit Record* (one of the two monthly magazines published in London for the Wine Trade) and who was a friend of ours, happened to be at my Evelyn Mansions flat for a chat and to see the children home from school. He was about to leave and I was with him in the hall when the bell rang. I opened the door. A burly messenger handed me a square white envelope and asked me to sign on his open delivery book my name on the dotted line. Then I shut the front door and tore open the white envelope. Incredible. It was Turner's Wine Book, the copy from the Huth Collection with the Ex-libris. There was a flimsy piece of paper with it, what used to be called a pro forma invoice; it gave you the price you would have to pay, should you decide to keep the book after due examination, but there was no obligation to buy the book. My shout of joy brought every-body into the hall, and Hugh took from my hand book, bill and envelope as I embraced my wife and told her how happy I was. Then it was that Hugh Cecil Lea, as he left the hall to step into the waiting lift, handed back to me my so precious book, and nothing else, 'This is my Christmas present to you. Don't bother about the bit of paper, I'll see to it!' he called out cheerfully. What a friend!

Many, I'm afraid, are the manuscripts and old books which I have bought but never read; I know where most of them are; I put them there with some well-meant promise that I would take them up and enjoy them when old age came and I would have time; little knowing that I would lose my sight. Bad enough, of course, but it might be worse; I still have my old books, and I love them still.

Love is blind!

XXII. NEARING THE END

MY dearly beloved wife died on 22 April 1963. We were married, in London, in 1900, having had to wait five years, three of military service and two while I got a job. We had loved one another, we had understood and helped one another the whole of our lives. Now the end had come. I had to have a change; a real change. I was only eighty-six, without a pain or an ache, quite as fit as men I knew who were twenty years younger. I had sold my Quarterly Magazine *Wine and Food* to Condé Nast, and I reckoned that I could afford to go round the world, mostly by sea to Australia and San Francisco, by air to New York, and by a Cunarder back to Southampton. This plan of mine, however, happened to be printed in the September 1963 *Wine and Food*, and when I reached Sydney, in December 1963, I found invitations from some of the American Wine and Food Societies, asking me to dine with them on my way from the Pacific to the Atlantic. It was so obvious to me that the cost of flying criss-cross about the U.S.A. would be greatly beyond my means that I declined them all without any hesitation, but I also promised them all that I would pay one last visit to the States, in 1966. I left it to them to decide where and when I was to come, but said I would be there for a few days, happy to meet any of the Society's Members from anywhere. Chicago in May 1966 was chosen, and I was there as promised. In the meantime I cancelled my cross-continent flight and my cross-Atlantic passage. I went back from Australia exactly the same way— a most comfortable way—as I had come to Australia, on the fine ship *Canberra*, with the same captain, the same cabin and the same cabin steward.

As I had never been to Australia and New Zealand before, I certainly got the change I wanted during some eight weeks in Australia, and over two in New Zealand. Vineyards, wineries, and wines were intensely interesting to me, and so was the scenery of the country and the lay-out of the cities, but it was the depth and sincerity of the kindness and affection of the friends I made which was the best tonic of all. As far as I knew I had but one friend in Australia when I landed at Sydney, Sir Jim McGregor, a dear friend of my wife's and myself for thirty years, but the kindness of Victor and Madge Gibson and so many more was wonderful, as was Frank Thorpy's in New Zealand!

On her February–March 1964 home voyage, *Canberra* remained tied to the dockside at her last port of call in Australia, Fremantle, on 28 February, my eighty-seventh birthday.

The Perth Wine and Food Society gave a first-class birthday lunch with wines and speeches galore, but I was not in the least anxious: *Canberra*'s captain was next to me and I knew that the *Canberra* would not sail without me!

A year later, my eighty-eighth birthday was something that I had never heard of or expected, let alone deserved. It lasted three days. On Saturday, 27 February 1965, the Guild of Wine Tasters of the Cape gave me a birthday's eve banquet in the banqueting chamber of the Cape Town City Hall; the next day, Sunday, the Cape Town Wine and Food Society gave me a Champagne birthday luncheon at Lanzerac, where I was staying as the guest of Sawfa (South Africa Wine Farmers' Association); and on the next day, Monday, 1 March, Sawfa gave a remarkable banquet at their Paarl headquarters. A gala performance deserving full marks! Zita Mulder, who looked after me on behalf of Sawfa, was so good that I called her—and still call her in writing—'my little mother'.

In May 1966 I flew from London to and back from Chicago to keep my appointment with my American friends—the first International Convention of the Wine and Food Society. I am glad that I did and am grateful that I was then still quite fit, although in my ninetieth year. Thanks to the energy, vision and optimism of Dr. George Rezek and a devoted team of hard-working helpers the Convention was a great success and it gave me much pleasure to see once more a few of my old American friends such as Roy Alciatore, all the way from New Orleans, Maynard Amerine from California, Paul Spitler and Harold Grossman, from New York, both of whom now are no more; as well as a number of younger friends from the U.S.A. and other parts of the world, including two delegates from Tokio. I was able to attend and enjoy luncheons, dinners and tastings like all delegates, talk as much as any of them, if not more.

In March 1967, when the old lease of my London flat came to an end, I decided to leave London and end my life at Little Hedgecourt with the two of my children who lived there. Back I went to gardening with a will and joy. There was much more to do than I could hope to do, but I did what I could and felt all the better for it, not realizing that it would not be for long.

It was in 1968 that old age caught me at last.

No complaints! I am ready to go. I have had more than my fair share of all that is best—faith, affection, and good health, three wonderful gifts that no money can buy.

I have worked hard as long as I could see, and loved it. Even when I can no longer see, I cannot accept idleness. I am still writing in the twilight.

BIBLIOGRAPHY

1905: HISTORY OF THE CHAMPAGNE TRADE IN ENGLAND.

First printed in monthly instalments in the *Wine Trade Review* (1904–5), and printed privately and poorly by Wyman at the expense of Lucien Loffet. It was sold at 5s. per copy for the benefit of the Wine and Spirit Trades' Benevolent Society.

1906: THE HISTORY OF THE WINE TRADE IN ENGLAND. Vol. I— The rise and progress of the Wine Trade in England from the earliest times to the end of the fourteenth century.

1907: As above. Vol. II—The progress of the Wine Trade in England during the fifteenth and sixteenth centuries. *Illustrated.*

1909: As above. Vol. III—The Wine Trade in England during the seventeenth century. *Illustrated.*

There is more hard work and original information in these three Volumes than in all my other books. They were printed at my expense by Wyman. Volume I was offered to the Wine Trade through the Wine Trade journals at 5s., its cost price, but it did not sell. Volumes II and III were offered for sale at 10s.; just as few (or as many) copies were sold, and as I only printed half the quantity of Volume I, odd copies of Volume I may still be bought today (1969) from second-hand booksellers, but copies of Volumes II and III have been practically unobtainable for many years.

1912: THE SEARCH AFTER CLARET.

A facsimile reprint from the copies in my library of three rare tracts published anonymously (by Richard Ames) in 1691. I wrote an Introduction and some 'Notes on Claret' for it and there were only fifty (numbered) copies printed at my expense by Palmer Sutton; they were given to friends and customers.

1912: MY FRENCH FRIEND. *A farce in one act.*

A small number of copies were printed at my expense by Palmer Sutton and sold for the benefit of the Wine and Spirit Trades' Benevolent Society on the evening of 9 February 1912, when this 'farce' was produced for the first and last time at the Royal Court Theatre, Sloane Square, by the Dramatic Society of the Wine Trade Club.

1913: IN VINO VERITAS. *London. Grant Richards.*

The first six lectures which I delivered at the Vintners' Hall during the winter months 1911–12. The same six lectures had previously been printed separately for distribution to the staff of provincial wine-merchants.

1913: BIBLIOTHECA VINARIA. *London. Grant Richards.*

A bibliography of books and pamphlets dealing with viticulture, wine-making, distillation, the management, sale, taxation, use and abuse of wine and spirits, in the newly formed library of the Wine Trade Club as well as in my own library. Only a very small number of copies were printed, and at my expense.

1915: GENERAL JOFFRE. *A popular life of the hero of the French nation. By a French Gunner. London. Simpkin Marshall. N.d.*

1915: LE MARECHAL FRENCH. *By A.L.S. Paris. Lethielleux. N.d.*

1915: LE GENERAL JOFFRE. *Par un artilleur français. Traduit de l'anglais par Christian de l'Isle. Paris. Lethielleux.*

The first two of these little books were written by me whilst at Vincennes during the winter of 1914, before I was accepted as an interpreter and sent to Le Havre in March 1915.

1916: SOMEWHERE IN FLANDERS. *N.d.*

A small geographical dictionary giving, in alphabetical order, the names (and some comments) of the various places where units of the 50th (Northumbrian) Division had been fighting or had been billeted during their first year of service overseas, April 1915 to March 1916. A publication without any name of author, of course, which was privately printed by Wyman against all rules and regulations; it was never offered for sale but distributed among my friends, and others, in the 50th Division.

1916: LAURIE'S ELEMENTARY RUSSIAN GRAMMAR. *By A.L.S. London. Werner Laurie. N.d.*

An escapist booklet written out of sheer desperation during the long winter of 1915, when dug-in in most depressing quarters outside Poperinghe. I sent it 'as a gift' to R. Eagle of Wyman & Sons, to do what he could with it: he gave it to Werner Laurie, who not only published it but sold the whole edition to the War Office. It became an 'issue' for all men who went or who were meant to be sent to Archangel.

1919: THE SALIENT, THE SOMME, AND ARRAS. *The Diary of a Bumble Bee. N.d.*

A diary and some reminiscences of the two years during which I was attached to the 50th (Northumbrian) Division, from April 1915 to April 1917. It was privately printed by Palmer Sutton and given at Christmas to my friends in and out of the 50th Division.

1919: FOOD AND DRINK. *London. The Wine Trade Club.*

The first of a series of 'educational' booklets to be written by me at the request of the Wine Trade Club Education Committee.

1919: ALCOHOL. *A Review of Lord d'Abernon's Book. London. The Wine Trade Club.* 1919.

The second of the Wine Trade Club's Education booklets; it was intended as a reply to *Alcohol: its action on the human organism*, a book of propaganda in favour of prohibition.

1919: WINE AND SPIRITS. *The Connoisseur's Textbook. London. Duckworth.*

Nineteen out of twenty-four chapters, dealing with various wines, spirits, beer, cider and even water, were originally published in 1913 and 1914 in Theodore Cook's monthly magazine *Land and Water*. The book was published on 2 October 1919, and was the first of my books to be 'published' in a business manner, and offered for sale to the public by booksellers in London and the Provinces.

1920: THE BLOOD OF THE GRAPE. *The wine trade text book. London. Duckworth.*

The substance of lectures which I delivered at the Vintner's Hall during the winter of 1919-20.

1920: LE LIVRE DE MON FILLEUL. *Lettres écrites pendant la guerre par un simple soldat à son filleul, le fils d'un de ses camarades de l'hiver* 1914–1915. *London. The Anglo-French Booksellers Ltd.* 1920.

My *filleul* was Georges Sivet, born in December 1914, *mon camarade* was his father, Eugène Sivet. The Anglo-French Booksellers Ltd. were one of Henry Davray's ventures.

1921: WINE AND THE WINE TRADE. *Illustrated. London. Sir Isaac Pitman & Sons. N.d.*

In Pitman's Common Commodities and Industries Series.

1923: THE SUPPLY, THE CARE AND THE SALE OF WINE: *a book of reference for wine-merchants. London. Duckworth.*

1923: LES PAUVRES DE FRANCE EN ANGLETERRE. *Croquis d'après nature. Illustrés par L. Bourgeoix-Borgex, Frank Brangwyn, R.A., Léon Carré, Bernard Naudin, Bernard Partridge, Poulbot, Louis Raemaekers, Jacques Simon, Steinlein and Willette. London. Duckworth. N.d.*

Printed at my expense and sold for the benefit of the French Benevolent Society.

1923: THE WINE CONNOISSEUR. *London. Wine Trade Club.*

Published by the Education Committee of the Wine Trade Club.

1924: THE ELIXIR OF YOUTH. *Notes on Champagne, Graves, Sauternes, Chablis, Hock and other White wines, still and sparkling. London. The Wine Trade Club.*
Published by the Education Committee of the Wine Trade Club.

1925: NOLITE TIMERE: *un cantique, quelques prières, et une lettre d'un père à ses enfants pour chaque jour de la semaine. London. Burns Oates & Washbourne Ltd.*

1926: ALMANACH DU FRANC BUVEUR POUR 1926. *Avec un frontispiece de Daragnes et 25 bois gravés. Paris. 'Le Livre.' Emile Chamontin. N.d.*
(En collaboration avec Léon Baranger.)

1926: BOTTLESCREW DAYS. *Illustrated. Wine drinking in England during the 18th Century. London. Duckworth.*
This was really Vol. IV of the *History of the Wine Trade in England.*

1927: BIBLIOTHECA BACCHICA. *Bibliographie raisonnée des ouvrages imprimés avant 1800 et illustrant la soif humaine sous tous ses aspects, chez tous les peuples, et dans tous les temps. Tome I. Incunables. London et Paris. Maggs Brothers. 1927.*
The edition was limited to 250 copies (numbered) and it was sold out within a year.

1928: THE BOLTON LETTERS. *The Letters of an English merchant in Madeira. 1695–1714. Vol. I. 1695–1700. London. Werner Laurie. N.d.*
A most interesting correspondence between William Bolton, at Madeira, and his London agent, Robert Heysham. I bought these Letters from Halliday, a Leicester bookseller, deciphered and typed them, and published the first batch (printed at my expense) but sold hardly any copies at all: the bulk of the edition, happily a small one, was pulped, and Vol. II was never published. Halliday bought back from me the Letters and I gave to Graham Blandy the typescript of the 1701–1714 Letters which had been prepared for Vol. II.

1929: PETIT DICTIONNAIRE DE POCHE FRANÇAIS-ANGLAIS, *à l'usage des Sommeliers. The Wine Butler's French-English Pocket Dictionary. N.d.*
Printed in Paris by l'Imprimerie du Griffon at the expense of l'Union des Sommeliers de Paris for distribution among their members.

1929: THE ART OF GOOD LIVING. *A Contribution to the better understanding of Food and Drink together with a Gastronomic Vocabulary and a Wine Dictionary. With a frontispiece after Daumier and a Foreword by Maurice Healy. London. Constable.*

1929: The same. Large paper and illustrated *Edition de luxe. London. Constable.*

1930: The same. *New York. Alfred Knopf.* 1930.

1931: WINE IN SHAKESPEARE'S DAYS AND SHAKESPEARE'S PLAYS. *N.d.*
This is No. 93 of the privately printed *Opuscula* of The Sette of Odd Volumes which were never sold but issued to all Members of the Sette.

1932: BIBLIOTHECA BACCHICA. *Tome II. Seizième siècle. London. Maggs Brothers.*
There were 275 numbered copies printed at my expense, of which 250 copies were sold in twenty-five years.

1933: MADEIRA: WINE, CAKES AND SAUCE. *London. Constable.*
In collaboration with Elizabeth Craig.

1933: TABLES OF CONTENT. *Leaves from my Diary. London. Constable.*

1934: CHAMPAGNE. *With Appendices on Corks; Methods of Keeping and Serving Champagne; Vintages; Brands; Shippers. London. Constable.*

1934: PORT. *London. Constable.*

1934: WINE AND THE WINE TRADE. *Second Edition. London. Sir Isaac Pitman. N.d.*

1934: THE WINE CONNOISSEUR'S CATECHISM. *London. Wine and Food Society.*

1935: WINES AND LIQUEURS FROM A TO Z. *A Glossary. London. The Wine and Food Society.*

1935: THE WINES OF FRANCE. *New York. The Wine and Food Society.*

1935: A DICTIONARY OF WINE. *With six maps. London. Cassell.*

1936: A CATECHISM CONCERNING CHEESES. *With a Glossary of cheeses and cheese dishes, and an introduction by Ernest Oldmeadow. London. The Wine and Food Society.*

1937: STAR CHAMBER REVELS (OR, THE FOUNTAYNE OF JUSTICE). *A Satyre acted on Friday, the eleventh of June, in the yeare 1602, by the then Lords of the Queene Elizabeth's most honourable Council. Peekskill, N.Y. The Watch Hill Press.*
275 copies hand-printed by James Hendrickson on antique paper.

1938: ANDRÉ SIMON'S FRENCH COOK BOOK. *Boston. Little, Brown.*

1938: THE CELLAR REGISTER. *Being a Bin Book wherein wine-lovers are conveniently enabled to record their judgement of the wines and spirits they have owned and the details of their purchase and consumption. London. The Wine and Food Society.*

The Curwen Press at their best.

1939: GERMAN WINES. *A classified List of the best Hocks and Moselles with notes upon German wines. Illustrated. London. The Wine and Food Society. N.d.*

Printed in Germany at the expense of the German Ministry of Agriculture.

1939: A CONCISE ENCYCLOPAEDIA OF GASTRONOMY. *Section I —Sauces. Comprising the principal classical sauce recipes together with a classified Index of condiments, garnishings, dressings, herbs, flavourings, seasonings and stuffings. London. The Wine and Food Society.*

1940: The same. *Section II—Fish. Comprising an Alphabetical List of edible Fishes, and a Selection of American, English and French Recipes for their culinary preparation and presentation. London. The Wine and Food Society.*

1941: The same. *Section III—Vegetables. Comprising an Alphabetical List of Vegetables, Herbs, Salads, Fungi, and edible weeds and a selection of American, English, French, Scottish and Welsh Recipes for their culinary preparation and presentation. London. The Wine and Food Society.*

1942: The same. *Section V—Fruit. Comprising an Alphabetical List of edible Fruits, with recipes for their culinary preparation; also an Index of Vegetables, Cereals, Fruits, Spices and Herbs recorded in Sections I, III, IV and V, together with their Latin or botanical names and the French or culinary titles of many of them; lastly, a Latin or botanical Index with corresponding English or Native names. London. The Wine and Food Society.*

1942: SOUPS. SALADS. SAUCES. *Wartime fare for the fastidious. With a foreword by Eugène Herbodeau and a postscript by Mrs. Jessop Hulton. London. The Wine and Food Society.*

1942: NO STARCH NO SUGAR. *Diabetic diet Miscellany. London. Hendebert Foods Co.*

1942: ALFRED D'ORSAY. *London. Franco-British Publishing Co.*

An account of Count d'Orsay's Life and of the French Benevolent Society founded by him in 1842. Published by the French Benevolent Society for its Centenary.

1943: THE SAINTSBURY CLUB. *A Scrap Book by the Cellarer.* *London. The Saintsbury Club.*
Privately printed for members of the Saintsbury Club.

1943: A CONCISE ENCYCLOPAEDIA OF GASTRONOMY. *Section IV—Cereals. Comprising an Alphabetical List of Cereals, Grasses, Plants and Trees, the seeds, roots, fruits or pith of which are made into flour, meal or paste for human consumption; together with the description of various flours and meals, and a number of recipes, both old and new, for the making of Bread, Biscuits and Cakes, Macaroni, Noodles and Spaghetti, Pastry and Pastries, etc.; also an analytical Table of Contents. London. The Wine and Food Society.*

1944: As above. *Section VI—Birds and their Eggs. Divided into three parts: The first of which deals with Game Birds and other Wild Fowl:—the second with utility Poultry; and the third with their eggs, both in the shell and in the dehydrated form. London. The Wine and Food Society.*

1944: NOTES ON THE LATE J. PIERPONT MORGAN'S CELLAR BOOK (1906). *London.*
Privately printed at The Curwen Press for members of the Saintsbury Club.

1944: WE SHALL EAT AND DRINK AGAIN. *A wine and food anthology. Edited by Louis Golding and André L. Simon. Illustrated by Zieglu. London. Hutchinson.*

1945: BASIC ENGLISH FARE. *London. Gramol.*

1945: A CONCISE ENCYCLOPAEDIA OF GASTRONOMY. *Section VII—Meat. Divided into two parts: The first part of which deals with butcher's meat, and the second with Mammals, other than the Ox, the Sheep and the Pig. London. The Wine and Food Society.*

1946: As above. *Section VIII—Wine, Beer, Cider, Spirits. Liqueurs, Cocktails, Cups, Mixed Drinks, Soft Drinks and Mineral Waters. London. The Wine and Food Society.*

1946: As above. *Section IX—Cheese: also an analytical cross-index to Sections I–VIII. London. The Wine and Food Society.*

1946: LET MINE BE WINE. *The philosophy of Wine. The anatomy of Wine. The geography of Wine. The choice of Wine. The service of Wine. London. The Wine and Food Society.*

1946: ENGLISH WINES AND CORDIALS. *London. Gramol.*

1946: VINTAGEWISE. *A Postscript to Saintsbury's* NOTES ON A CELLAR BOOK. *London. Michael Joseph.*

1947: MADEIRA AND ITS WINES. *Illustrated. Funchal. Issued by Madeira Wine Association Lda., Madeira.*

1948: ANDRÉ SIMON'S FRENCH COOK BOOK. *New edition revised by Crosby Gaige. Boston. Little, Brown.*

An entirely Americanized production which is a caricature of the original (1938) edition.

1948: DRINK. *The pleasures of life series. Illustrated. London. Burke Publishing Co.*

1949: FOOD. *The pleasures of life series. Illustrated. London. Burke Publishing Co.*

1949: A CALENDAR OF FOOD AND WINE. *Compiled by Nell Heaton and André Simon, with illustrations by T. B. L. Huskinson. London. Faber & Faber.*

1949: A DICTIONARY OF GASTRONOMY. *London. The Wine and Food Society.*

This is the only really bad book published by the Wine and Food Society. So many copies were faulty and had to be replaced that I sent most of the print to be pulped and refused to sell any more.

1949: As above. *New York. Farrar, Straus & Co.*

The same Manchester-printed sheets were sent to New York and bound there by Farrar, Straus & Co. but they found it impossible to sell anything like the number of copies which they had bought: and they never were expected nor asked to pay for them.

1949: IN PRAISE OF GOOD LIVING. *An anthology for friends. London. Frederick Muller.*

1949: PRACTICAL COOKERY FOR ALL. *London. Odham's Press.*

I contributed all Wine entries in this book: cookery, by far the more important part of the book, was dealt with by Blanche Anding, Gwenneth Chappell, Lydia Chatterton and Jessie Lindsay.

1950: THE WINES OF THE WORLD POCKET LIBRARY:
1. Champagne
2. Port
3. Sherry
4. South African wines
5. Claret
6. Graves and Sauternes
7. Burgundy
8. Hocks & Moselles
9. Brandy
10. Rum.

London. The Wine and Food Society.

1951: As above:

    11. Madeira

    12. Italy

    13. Yugoslavia

    14. Switzerland and Luxembourg

    15. California

    16. Alsace, Arbois and the Loire Valley

    17. The Rhône, Provence, Languedoc and Roussillon.

London. The Wine and Food Society.

1951: THE ART OF GOOD LIVING. *With a foreword by Sir Francis Meynell. London. Michael Joseph Ltd.*

A revised edition of *The Art of Good Living* published by Constable in 1929, with a foreword by Maurice Healy.

1951: MUSHROOMS GALORE. *A Book of Mushroom recipes. Introduction by F. C. Atkins, Chairman of the Mushroom Growers Association of Great Britain and Northern Ireland. London. Newman Neame.*

Danish edition 1952.

1951: PARTNERS. *A guide to the game of Wine and Food matchmaking. London. The Wine and Food Society.*

1952: THE GOURMET'S WEEK-END BOOK. *With decorations by Beryl Irving. London. Seeley Service.*

1952: A CONCISE ENCYCLOPAEDIA OF GASTRONOMY. *With decorations by John Leigh-Pemberton. Complete and unabridged. London. Collins.*

1952: As above. *New York. Harcourt, Brace Co.*

The original *Encyclopaedia*'s nine sections published in one volume with an Index.

1952: HOW TO SERVE WINE IN HOTELS AND RESTAURANTS. *London. Newman Neame.*

1952: HOW TO ENJOY WINE IN THE HOME. *London. Newman Neame.*

1952: WINES AND LIQUEURS FROM A TO Z. *A Glossary. London. The Wine and Food Society.*

A revised edition of one of the most popular publications of the Wine and Food Society.

German edition 1960.

1953: WHAT ABOUT WINE? *All the Answers. Wood-engravings by David Gentleman. London. Newman Neame.*

1953: BIBLIOTHECA GASTRONOMICA. *A Catalogue of books and*

M

documents on gastronomy compiled and annotated, with an Introduction by André L. Simon. The production, taxation, distribution, and consumption of food and drink: their use and abuse in all times and among all peoples. London. The Wine and Food Society.

Edition limited to 750 numbered copies. Maggs Brothers dealt with trade orders and sold nearly 400 copies in three years.

1955: ENGLISH FARE AND FRENCH WINE. *London. Newman Neame.*

1956: CHEESES OF THE WORLD. *London. Faber & Faber.*

1956: KNOW YOUR WINES. *London. Coram.*

1956: THE WINE AND FOOD MENU BOOK. *London. Frederick Muller.*

1957: THE WINES OF FRANCE. *Paris. Comité National de propagande en faveur du vin.*

A revised and enlarged edition of the booklet first published in 1935 by the Wine and Food Society, at the expense of the Comité de Propagande, for free distribution in the U.S.A.

1956: A WINE PRIMER. *A text-book for beginners on how to buy, keep and serve wine. (Revised edition.) London. Michael Joseph.*
German edition 1965.

1957: BY REQUEST. *An autobiography. London. The Wine and Food Society.*

1957: THE NOBLE GRAPES AND GREAT WINES OF FRANCE. *With 24 coloured plates by Percy Hennell, maps and illustrations. New York and London. McGraw-Hill.*

1958: LET WINE BE MINE. *London. The Wine and Food Society.*

1958: A DICTIONARY OF WINES AND LIQUEURS. *London. Herbert Jenkins.*
German edition 1960. Revised edition 1961.

1960: ANDRÉ SIMON'S GUIDE TO GOOD FOOD AND WINE. *A Concise Encyclopaedia of Gastronomy. (Revised edition.) London. Collins.*

1961: MENUS FOR GOURMETS. *London. Herbert Jenkins. New York. Hearthside Press.*

1962: THE HISTORY OF CHAMPAGNE. *London. George Rainbird. New York. McGraw-Hill.*
German edition 1962. Dutch edition 1964. Italian edition 1968.

1963: THE GREAT WINES OF GERMANY (*with F. S. Hallgarten*). *London and New York. McGraw-Hill.*

1964: THE HISTORY OF THE WINE TRADE IN ENGLAND. *3 vols. Illustrated. Reproduced from three volumes originally published in 1906/8.*

1966: THE COMMONSENSE OF WINE. *London. George Rainbird.* Swedish edition 1968.

1966: THE WINES, VINEYARDS AND VIGNERONS OF AUSTRALIA. *Melbourne. Lansdowne.*

SOME LECTURES AND ADDRESSES WHICH HAVE BEEN PUBLISHED

Wine and the Wine Trade in England. Retrospect and prospect. A lecture delivered at the Vintners' Hall, on 11 October 1932, under the auspices of the Education Committee of the Wine Trade Club. London. Crozier Press. 1932.

Wine and the Wine Trade. A paper read at the thirteenth Congress of the *Ligue Internationale des adversaires de la prohibition*, at Vintners' Hall, London, June 1933.

The value of wine. Address to the Hotelkeepers Conference, Bournemouth, 1934.

Vendanges et Vin. B.B.C. French Talks. *The Listener.* 21 October 1936. *The art of good living.* A lecture delivered at The Royal Society of Arts, 15 December 1937. *Journal of the R.S.A.* No. 4440. 24 December 1937.

Unusual Vegetables. A lecture delivered at The Royal Horticultural Society. 12 April 1938. *Journal of the R.H.S.* Vol. LXIII. Part 6. 1938.

Wine, leisure and personality. Address to the Hotelkeepers Conference, Southport. 1938.

Wine: to know and to serve. Lecture delivered at the First Management refresher Course of the Hotels and Restaurants Association. London. January 1948.

Wine makes the meal. Address to the Hotelkeepers Conference, Harrogate. October 1950.

ARTICLES, NOTES AND OBITUARY
NOTICES IN *WINE AND FOOD*

ARTICLES AND NOTES

OBITUARY NOTICES

INDEX

INDEX